Creative Drama and Music Methods

Creative Drama and Music Methods

Activities for the Classroom

THIRD EDITION

Janet E. Rubin and Margaret Merrion

ROWMAN & LITTLEFIELD PUBLISHERS, INC.

Lanham • Boulder • New York • Toronto • Plymouth, UK

Published by Rowman & Littlefield Publishers, Inc.
A wholly owned subsidiary of The Rowman & Littlefield Publishing Group, Inc.
4501 Forbes Boulevard, Suite 200, Lanham, Maryland 20706
http://www.rowmanlittlefield.com

Estover Road, Plymouth PL6 7PY, United Kingdom

British Library Cataloguing in Publication Information Available

Library of Congress Cataloging-in-Publication Data
Rubin, Janet.
    Creative drama and music methods : activities for the classroom / by Janet E. Rubin and
Margaret Merrion. — 3rd ed.
        p. cm.
    Includes index.
    ISBN 978-1-4422-0461-4 (cloth : alk. paper) —
    ISBN 978-1-4422-0462-1 (pbk. : alk. paper) —
    ISBN 978-1-4422-0463-8 (electronic)
    1. Drama in education. 2. Music in education. 3. Improvisation (Acting) 4. Movement
(Acting) 5. Children's theater. I. Merrion, Margaret Dee. II. Title.
PN3171.R75 2011
372.13'32—dc22   2010036133

Printed in the United States of America

We dedicate this book to
our loving families and loyal friends
for their boundless affection and support.

Contents

Chapter 3

Chapter 4

Preface

THIS THIRD EDITION OF *CREATIVE DRAMA AND MUSIC METHODS* has several new features. We based the improvements on suggestions from teachers who seek to integrate the arts easily and frequently. This edition integrates more core curriculum. To aid the teacher who uses the activities directly from the book, sidebars with succinct directions and ideas are offered for ease in accessing information.

Web resources have been added; music literature and dramatic literature have been updated. Many more activities are included, with suggested grade levels for each category. With additional materials and activities, chapter contents have been restructured to assure a sequential continuum of growth.

Terminology is explained in the context of the activities, as well as in the glossary, to help teachers with limited background in creative drama and music. New lessons have been developed for the conclusion of each chapter. Finally, reflection questions suitable for journal exploration have been designed into an appendix.

We trust these improvements will lead to more success and joy in integrating creative drama and music into your methods.

Janet E. Rubin
Margaret Merrion

Acknowledgments

- Ann Garcia
- Jeff Hall
- Saginaw Valley State University
- Susan Corak
- Western Michigan University

We wish to gratefully acknowledge the many fine teachers, colleagues, and students whose ideas, activities, questions, and love of the arts have shaped this book. After years as learners and teachers, we are no longer always able to match contributions to specific individuals, but we value and thank all who have influenced and assisted us.

CHAPTER 1

Creative Drama and Music in Instructional Settings

CREATIVITY AND INNOVATION ARE receiving significant attention as global, technological, economic, and industrial forces cause changes at breakneck speed, from third-world to the most advanced civilizations. To sustain progress, businesses, as well as nonprofit organizations, seek the keys to go from "good to great." Both conventional wisdom and recent research point to the power of imagination, risk taking, and creativity for success. These are not new concepts, for all human beings have creative potential within themselves. We welcome the resurgence of attention—especially attention in education—to this critical facet of personal and societal development. And creativity all starts with the growth of one human being: a baby!

Healthy babies are innately curious, inquisitive explorers. They set out to discover the world through their senses. Their awareness of the world grows through the things they see, hear, smell, feel, and taste. As soon as they are skilled enough to grasp objects, they examine them closely by feeling them, tasting them, shaking them, and even smelling them. Once they are crawling and walking, they can begin to explore their world.

But this spirit of adventure is dampened with admonitions as the child grows older: "Don't do that." "NO!" "Don't touch." "Stay out." "Keep off." "Don't go near

that." The child soon learns some limits. Happily, at certain junctures in childhood, a resurgence of the spirit of adventure occurs. For instance, when a child gets a new bike, suddenly unfamiliar parts of the neighborhood warrant exploration; or a fishing pole may lead to the discovery of new creeks. Overall, however, innate curiosity is curbed over time. In classrooms nationwide, teachers sadly report that when children begin formal schooling, it is challenging to motivate them to explore, to discover, and to satisfy curiosity. Worse, the older a child gets, the more inhibition may be displayed. The natural desire to learn has diminished.

Something is wrong when an innate, desirable characteristic—a natural ability that could serve a child well throughout a lifetime—is not positively reinforced. In part, this may be due to a serious omission in the education of many children. Simply put, while there appears to be an appropriate emphasis on the cognitive and psychomotor aspects of development, there is a serious neglect of the affective aspects of growth. The affective areas such as initiative, independence, interests, attitudes, and feelings (e.g., wonder, surprise, joy, disappointment, grief) must have a place in childhood education. They are part of the wholeness of being human.

There is no question that education must help children learn to take their places in society. And much of that preparation involves formal schooling to develop skills for clear thinking, reading, writing, and computing, and ultimately for making a living. There is some question, however, concerning what sort of preparation children need along with survival skills and job training. For example, learning how to make a living does not necessarily involve learning how to make a life. People are more than workers. In order to enhance not only work but all life experiences, the *whole* child must be educated.

This educational responsibility is sometimes easier to understand than to implement. Teachers are under pressure from administrators and parents to make sure that students' standardized test scores are satisfactory. The teaching style may default to "teaching to the test." This may achieve short-term goals, but it risks forfeiting the view that the child should be a lifelong learner who needs many ways to access information.

As participants in creative drama and music, children will explore their creative potential as human beings—that is, the potential with which they are born. They will also approach the learning of other content (math, science, language arts, and so forth) through approaches that naturally integrate creative arts for successful outcomes. These creative activities allow children to discover a wide range of new knowledge and feelings within themselves. Just as babies touch, listen, shake, taste, and smell new objects to acquire knowledge and form attitudes, students of all ages will use the creative arts to continue this discovery journey into adulthood.

Recognizing that students have various skills and may already prefer different learning styles, educators must identify how children best acquire learning. Much formal knowledge is presented (and tested) in a verbal format. Consequently, students spend a disproportionate amount of time sitting at desks, reading, writing, doing word problems, and following written directions. While all students must develop strong verbal skills, no one learning style will equally suit each child in the class. Some will learn well by rote (through oral/aural presentation of information). Still others will grasp content tactically (manipulating objects, using a keyboard) or kinesthetically (moving). With visual imagery so pervasive (through technology and other media), children would do well to develop diverse learning styles, so as to be facile and successful for whatever the future challenges of learning hold. Thus, the experiences teachers provide should incorporate a variety of learning opportunities for each student, regardless of stylistic abilities and preferences.

MERGING THEORY AND PRACTICE

This book offers instruction that reaches students in a variety of ways. It is grounded in the belief that all children can be successful students if learning activities engage them and offer them more than mundane classroom experiences. Discovery, surprise, and fun are fundamental to a meaningful education. Creative drama and music activities honor the gifts that young people innately possess and that can be their gateway to active and lifelong learning.

This is not a typical creative drama or music text. First, it takes a process approach to the two arts. This means that of primary significance is the value that the child gains from the experience. This also may mean that although what the child produces is not of finished performance caliber, it may be reflective of personal growth. Some degree of success is achievable by all participants regardless of the level of talent. The process approach respects the artistic intelligence of the child. The growth and development of the person are of greater significance here than the artistic outcome. These activities are child centered rather than audience centered. We focus on creative drama and musical activities because both art forms are display arts and both have high potential for generating creative self-expression.

Second, this text advocates natural methods of learning. The approach is based on discovery and participation. The thesis is that experiential learning produces direct and lasting results. The activities in this book involve primarily "natural resources" in the process of learning. Natural resources include a desire to explore, physical freedom, spontaneity, imagination, empathic response, curiosity, movement from self-centered to more social interactions, sensory awareness, listening and speaking skills, and the appreciation of each person's uniqueness.

Third, coverage of content is appropriate for both the elementary and middle school years. This is an optimal period of growth and development. It is a time to explore one's self and one's world with a sense of wonder and freedom. This is a perfect opportunity to foster self-expression and exploration through creative drama and music.

Fourth, the activities that follow lend themselves to being comfortably incorporated into classroom routine and place no additional burdens on the teacher. These are designed for educators with valid learning objectives but limited experience

in creative drama and music. This book is designed to serve as a primer for the novice. Success here may indeed provide motivation to seek additional and deeper experiences in these arts.

Finally, the material in this book is fun to use. Enjoyment should be a fundamental part of growing up and learning. In the following pages, there is a deliberate inclusion of activities that children find meaningful, thought-provoking, imaginative, and *fun*!

TERMINOLOGY AND ROLES

The terms **leader** and **players** are used throughout this text to refer, respectively, to the person conducting the activity and to the children (lower- and upper-level students). The leader has certain responsibilities, such as preparing the lesson, building and maintaining a creative climate, pacing activities, determining when sufficient planning and practice have occurred, helping the players extract meaning from the process, and assessing the outcomes.

Because leading creative learning may be a new role for some leaders, aspects of that role are worth reviewing. Experience affirms the importance of the leader being a coexplorer and full participant in activities. This means that the inquisitive, curious, risk taking part of the leader's nature should be reawakened and nurtured, and that imagination, sensitivities, and creativity will come into play. Fun is in store for the leader, too.

There is no standard format for leader participation. Not all leaders possess the same degree of willingness or ability to participate in each activity. It is important, however, that the leader be authentic in the process. Some will participate fully, involving themselves wholeheartedly with each activity. Others may be involved only as guides. Still others may find that they observe some activities and participate in others. Regardless of approach, each leader should be open to experiencing personal growth, much as is expected of the players. The leader also should model positive involvement in the experience. Children are perceptive and they will recognize false enthusiasm. The leader's comfortable participation in many ways validates the experience and communicates respect for the arts and for creative risk taking . Thus, a "teaching distance" should be avoided when conducting creative activities.

Lower level (K–4) and upper level (5–8) designations are recommended throughout the text. This guides the leader in determining age-appropriate activities. Often a specific activity can be appropriate throughout the range of grade levels if the content and complexity are adjusted to the cognitive and physical skill levels. The leader will be introduced to specific terminology regarding creative drama and music through boldface words. The definitions will be presented within the context of the activity as well as referenced in the glossary for additional clarification.

GETTING STARTED

To begin, simple activities are introduced. As players become more competent and comfortable, more difficult activities can be presented. Often the beginning activities serve as foundations for later ones. It is not necessary that players experience each and every activity; however, leaders are likely to find more success if some activities are approached on a graduated basis. While leaders will recognize that the activities can be used in an order other than the one presented in the text, this progression is recommended.

PREPARING SUCCESSFUL LESSONS

Beginning leaders should be aware that, in creative drama and music activities, there may not be a "right" answer. The open nature of the experience may produce multiple appropriate responses. Students, for example, may give diverse "right" answers or creative interpretations. Leaders and players more familiar with standardization may find this concept difficult, but what one leader may identify as "right" in an activity may not be the choice of another. What is important is that decisions about divergent responses be supported in ways that match the leader's intentions for the activity.

A key concept for the leader is that of focusing on a limited number of objectives for each lesson and concentrating on realizing them. Lesson planning should be guided by the questions, "What will the students learn?" and "How will this learning be recognized?" Many outcomes may be possible and legitimate, but energy is best directed toward identifying, achieving, and assessing a limited number.

The leader is encouraged to begin incorporating creative drama and music activities into lessons on a structured and planned basis. This will help both leader and players become acquainted with and comfortable with their use. Those leaders, for example, who work with children regularly may find it desirable to plan short lessons centered on a theme or topic the players are studying. In this way, integration of arts into other core curriculum is natural, nonthreatening, and nonintrusive. Once students are accustomed to this approach, they are likely to want longer sessions and to seek opportunities for spontaneously infusing arts into lessons. As leaders become accustomed to working with creative drama and music, they will become sensitive to unstructured opportunities for incorporating the forms into teaching. The chance to integrate a rhythm echo, for example, to get the group's attention will present itself and work naturally within the environment. It is hoped that leaders will apply these activities in both structured settings and informal circumstances that arise. The activities are so useful that leaders will readily see their value and develop a knack for including them.

CONTENT AND ACHIEVEMENT STANDARDS

Just as with other content areas, the arts have standards that describe knowledge and skills as well as expected outcomes for each discipline. Standards address what students should know and be able to do in the arts and specify the understandings and levels of achievement that students are expected to attain. Please see artsedge.kennedy-center.org/teach/standards for additional information.

PATTERNS OF PROGRESSION

In creative drama and music, the leader will recognize several **patterns of progression**. One such pattern moves from short to long lessons. Early sessions, for example, may consist of one short activity lasting a few minutes. As players become more skilled and their interest in the material grows, sessions are likely to become longer. A second pattern moves from unison play to individual play. **Unison play** is prevalent in beginning sessions as children play the activities together. In advanced lessons, there may be more opportunities for **individual play** or solo work. A third pattern moves from teacher-directed to student-directed activities. As participants gain skills and confidence, they take more responsibility for the content. **Teacher-directed** sessions

are more often associated with beginning lessons, while **student-directed** sessions are associated with more complex arts experiences. These patterns suggest the fourth, which is movement from simple to complex activities. Note that more than one pattern may be operational in any given session.

Special attention should be given to the simple-to-complex pattern in creative drama as it pertains to skill development. The movement from beginning activities to story dramatization is based on a hierarchical progression. Simple beginning activities establish a comfortable playing climate and introduce the format. Pantomime activities focus upon the body, helping players to develop the physical skills needed for later characterization. Improvisation allows them to add vocal dimension and quick thinking ability to physical responses. **Story creation** often has roots in improvisation and integrates literary components and dramatic structure into already acquired skills. Having familiarity with story work, players bring all of their abilities together in story dramatization, which unifies elements from the previous levels. The pyramid in figure 1.1 illustrates the structure.

THE IMPORTANCE OF ARTS EDUCATION

In the twenty-first century, young people require an education that addresses the whole child. Today's learner will need to acquire critical thinking and creative competencies. The workplace will demand skills in problem solving, innovation, adaptation, working collaboratively, demonstrating initiative, productivity, taking responsibility, and leadership. The complex world in which today's students will live requires that they communicate clearly, understand social and cultural

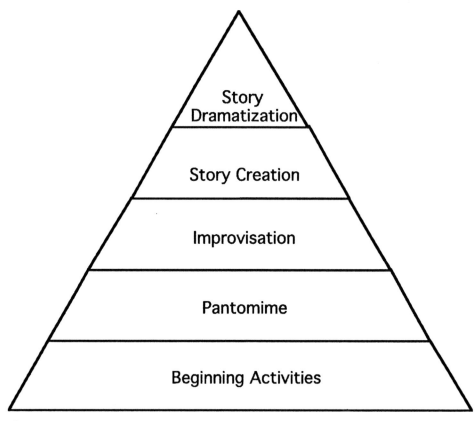

Story
Dramatization

Story Creation

Improvisation

Pantomime

Beginning Activities

Figure 1.1

contexts, and have the ability to be flexible in the face of challenging and changing circumstances. The arts give students opportunities to develop and refine these critical skills.

Why, then, has the struggle to include the arts in many classrooms been so difficult? One pressing reason has been the increasing demand upon teachers to make sure that students do well on standardized tests. This has resulted in a priority, in many classrooms, to teach to the test and to exclude other content. Further, in some cash-strapped school districts there is a fear that the incorporation of the arts will require additional hiring of arts professionals. While this is clearly desirable, there are activities such as those in

this text that can be successfully led by the classroom teacher. The arts can profoundly affect learning, and the arts can be instrumental in educating for success, both as discipline-specific content and in partnership with other curricula.

Teachers can turn to research by foundations and professional organizations for evidence of the benefits of arts education. The Dana Foundation, for example, has sponsored summits and posted research on its website (www.dana.org) noting connections between arts training and learning, cognition, focus on task, memory, creative thinking, and general intelligence. Examples such as the following illustrate findings relating directly to the arts showcased in this text: (1) training in music correlates with the ability to differentiate and manipulate sounds, a predictor of reading fluency, and (2) training in drama/theatre suggests better social skills, increased motivation, and improved memory. Another connection addresses equity, as socioeconomically disadvantaged students have benefited significantly from arts education experiences. On the website and in publications of the Arts Education Partnership (aep-arts.org), resources and research further the case for the arts. AEP's mission centers on the essential role of the arts in students' success. In addition to the Dana Foundation and AEP, many other professional organizations, government agencies, foundations, and research institutes are sources for arts education support and advocacy. Anecdotal evidence also abounds, not the least of which is the heartfelt testimony of students whose lives have been enriched through the arts.

Keeping students in school and having them do well is critical to their success. The arts play an active role on these fronts. The Center for Arts Education, for example, released a report noting that those New York City high schools that had the highest graduation rates also provided students with the most access to arts education, while those with the lowest rates provided the least access. Noting that, according to the U.S. Department of Education, fewer than seven out of ten students graduate from high school on time and 1.3 million leave high school without a diploma each year, Sandra S. Ruppert states the case for the importance of arts education in schools:

> We know that the arts can make a difference in the academic lives of 8th graders. A decade ago, the Arts Education Partnership published ground-breaking research that compared 8th graders who were highly involved in the arts with those who had little or no involvement, and found consistently better outcomes for the highly involved students: better grades, less likelihood of dropping out by grade 10, and more positive attitudes about school. The study also showed that the benefits of high levels of arts participation can make more of a difference for economically disadvantaged students.[1]

The arts engage students in ways that other subjects may not, providing ways into learning that complement learning styles and encourage creative risk taking. The arts are process oriented, facilitate inquiry, and promote self-expression. Through the arts, children can see themselves as creators who value their own ideas and respect the ideas of others. This gateway to learning helps them understand that there is not always a right answer to a question, or that there may be multiple ways to address a problem. The arts allow them to learn both from their successes and from their mistakes. The positive results are tangible, both in terms of arts content learning and in the ability to understand and communicate meaning across disciplines. In addition, the arts can make positive social changes as they open doors to knowledge. Through arts experiences, students' talents are nurtured as their potential is realized.

Arguments that incorporating the arts will take time away from the study of other subjects lack validity. The arts enhance learning and support student achievement. Improvements in math, reading, writing, communication, and literacy have ties to arts education. Behavior such as being attentive, completing homework, and volunteering in class are fostered through arts education experiences. Students learn to plan, sequence, analyze, select, and evaluate with a purpose when it comes to their creative work.

Children deserve a chance to know themselves—their talents, their emotional selves, their attitudes, their fears, their joys—and to experience academic, social, and creative success. Students need opportunities to express themselves through the arts. When willing participants, a skilled leader, and engaging learning materials are present, conditions are most favorable for personal, academic, social, and artistic growth.

ARTS EDUCATION EXPERIENCES

- improve academic performance;
- result in better attendance and lower dropout rates;
- level the playing field for students from disadvantaged socioeconomic backgrounds;
- build self-esteem;
- foster self-confidence and self-expression;
- improve academic and performance skills for children with learning disabilities;
- improve literacy skills;
- foster motivation;
- create empathy for and understanding of others;
- improve oral and written communication skills.

GUIDELINES FOR SUCCESS

Creative climates involve freedom to explore and experience, but they also involve parameters. While acknowledging that no two groups are the same and that each leader is the best judge of how to facilitate creative conditions, the following guidelines will be helpful in meeting the goals of creative drama and music lessons.

1. Recognize variables. Much that will occur in a creative drama or music session may be spontaneous and unpredictable. Two variables, however, can be anticipated. These are (a) group dynamics and (b) the timing needed for creative planning and adaptive response.

   Each group of players is unique. Many factors determine the character of the group. First, there is the group itself and how well the children know and work with each other. Then, there is the group interaction with the leader. Influencing this aspect will be familiarity with each other and degrees of trust and confidence. Also weighing into the mix are past experiences of players and leader, both positive and negative, as well as the creative climate within a particular session. The leader should recognize that one activity may work well with one group and fail with another. Group dynamics can influence play either subtly or overtly.

   A second variable relates to the fact that, when conducting creative experiences, exact timing and mood are difficult to predict. The duration of an activity, for example, may change if open-ended responses and group decision making develop beyond the allotted time. Or an activity may evolve in a different direction, requiring the leader to adapt the lesson plan. Mood, material selected, and events either within or outside of the classroom can influence the timing.

2. Build in "think" time. If the activity involves large group responses, then timing should be gauged ac-

cordingly. With individual play, a player may need thinking time as well. It is a good idea to give the whole group a minute or two to prepare several ideas, in case one player suggests another's idea before his or her turn arrives. The leader should allow adequate time for preparation and participation.

3. Organize play. Checking with groups as they plan ensures that their ideas are suited to the activity, can be done safely, and will not embarrass others. The leader can always ask for **preview play** to see what the players plan to present.

   Players always should be encouraged to respond and be given ample time to do so. Care should be taken, however, to prevent players who are unable to think of or share responses from feeling embarrassed. Insisting on or forcing participation is counterproductive to maintaining a creative climate.

4. Lead the activity with sensitivity. Leaders who are responsive to the momentum of the activity and the behavior of the group recognize signs of fatigue, disinterest, confusion, or bafflement. One rule of thumb is to stop an activity *before* it is overdone. Even when the players wish to continue, replay, or go to another activity, it is better to close the experience on an enjoyable note—whetting appetites for more—than let it run too long and risk boredom or silliness.

   If players do become tired or lose interest during the session, the leader should not be discouraged, but should look closely at what went wrong. Perhaps the same activity would be more successful if replayed at another time or with a few changes. Activities can be reintroduced when the group's mood or the creative climate becomes more favorable. The leader can also revert to simpler activities at any time.

   If **pacing** is a problem, the leader should determine if activities were explained or played too quickly. Players may become confused or frustrated if directions have been given too rapidly, energy has lagged, or the goal of the activity is unclear.

5. Be open. There may be a real temptation, particularly with early experiences, to predetermine responses in order to guarantee success. As this may happen unintentionally, the leader should be especially alert and guard against it. Whether consciously planned or not, this mindset may limit creative responses. Some leaders may have to learn to withhold personal responses in order to allow the players to offer theirs. This requires the leader to be flexible, adaptive, and capable of discarding ideas when play moves in a valid, but unanticipated, direction.

6. Temper openness with safety and fair play. Creative response and chaos are not the same things, and the leader needs to be clear about the difference. Some experimentation will likely be in order to find an appropriate method of classroom management (which is discussed in more detail in chapter 3).

7. Be prepared. Before beginning, review the desired outcomes, mentally rehearse the activity, and learn about the players. Practice the lesson out loud to enhance the fluency of presentation and stimulate greater interaction.

   Anticipating students' questions, assessing their prior knowledge, and considering questions that might arise are useful techniques. Making sure the questions stimulate creative thinking helps establish the climate and purpose of the lesson. By anticipating players' responses, the leader may avoid problems during the actual lesson.

It is also a good idea to prepare a list of questions that moves the lesson forward. Good questions are **open-ended** and ensure that the activities stimulate creative thought. Asking, for example, "How does the **character** feel?" will generate more creative thinking than the **closed question**, "Is the character happy?" which requires only a yes or no response. Answers to questions also may provide assessment.

8. Step aside. The goal of any activity is to build creative competencies. Therefore, the leader will want to anticipate ways for players to further an activity once it has been introduced. As players become comfortable and confident, they will want more responsibility for directing the session. When they are ready to do so, the leader need give only a framework or minimal guidance.

Creative drama and music activities can enliven the classroom environment and enrich learning experiences. The skills that are fostered reach beyond these arts; they are life skills that generate confidence, curiosity, and creative risk taking in learners. As educators incorporate the content that follows into their personal teaching styles, it is hoped that they will realize the power of the arts as resources and partners in preparing young people for a promising future.

NOTE

1. Sandra S. Ruppert, "Why Schools with Arts Programs Do Better at Narrowing Achievement Gaps," online commentary, *Education Week* 29, no. 5 (September 23, 2009).

CHAPTER 2

Beginning Activities

To begin a session, the leader should seek activities that create interest and foster relaxation and trust. Activities can be done individually, or several activities can constitute a lesson. These need not be related by theme or topic, but this is sometimes done for organizational purposes and may be a useful way to approach content integration.

Selecting or designing **beginning activities** that appeal to both the leader and the players is the first step in creating a successful lesson. In early sessions, everyone might feel unsure, nervous, and concerned about what is expected. Students may need reassurance that what they are about to do is both enjoyable and nonthreatening. A sense of adventure is helpful here. Simple beginning activities will help everyone relax, and the leader's self-assurance can grow along with the players' confidence.

Please note that beginning activities, as well as most creative drama and music exercises, can be adapted for different grade levels. Once leaders understand the format for an activity, they can create materials that will specifically work for their players.

ICE-BREAKERS (LOWER/UPPER LEVELS)

Name Tags or Tent Cards

Knowing the names of the players will not only help put them at ease, but will facilitate pacing and help the leader establish a supportive classroom climate. Players like to be addressed by name, and doing so helps establish rapport. This is particularly helpful in situations where players know one another but the leader is new to them. Calling players by name is immediately inclusive and helps spark and maintain their interest.

Learning names can be undertaken in a creative fashion and can be made a part of the session through purposefully designed activities and devices. This approach is imaginative and enjoyable and will help get the session off to a good start.

If a roster is available, name tags or tent cards (self-standing nameplates, often made of strong paper, tag board, or poster board) can be constructed, and names filled in, before meeting with the participants. If necessary, names can be filled in at the start of the session, although with a large group this can be time-consuming. If a session is to be theme-related, name tags or tent cards can help set the tone for the activities. A creative drama lesson centered on a circus theme, for example, might call for name tags in the shape of balloons or clowns, while one dealing with autumn might use leaf shapes. Tent cards might incorporate these designs in a colorful border. If the session is comprised of a series of unrelated activities, more generic pieces are suggested. More advanced participants can design their own tags or tents, using original art and signatures.

Content can be cleverly incorporated in name tags or tents as well. Players always enjoy tags or tent cards in the shapes of animals (science), video game or cartoon characters (language arts alliteration, such as "Bugs Bunny"), or geometric figures such as circles and triangles (math).

Name Games

Name games function as ice-breakers designed to relax the participants and establish a positive climate for creative work. For these activities, it is suggested that the leader and players sit in a circle. The leader begins each activity, providing an example for participants as well as communicating interest in the game.

NAME GAME: LETTER MATCHING. Going around the circle, players state their names, each one mentioning something he or she likes that begins with the same letter as his or her first name.

Examples:
My name is Alice, and I like apples.
My name is Bill, and I like balloons.

When used with young players, this activity can be an effective means of integrating language arts into the session. A leader can check for comprehension of letter recognition and alliteration.

Example:
My name is Colleen, and I like kites.

Upon hearing this, the leader will realize that Colleen is having difficulty distinguishing between the letters *c* and *k*. The leader should avoid focusing on the error

but ought to address it in later instruction. If other players call attention to it, the leader acknowledges the mistake and then continues the name game.

NAME GAME: VARIATION 1. Going around the circle, players couple their names with things they like. In this variation, the item the player likes need not begin with the first letter of the first name. The focus here is more on recognition of the player's interests than on letter recognition.

Example:
My name is Harry, and I like pizza.

NAME GAME: VARIATION 2. In this variation, the player's interest is related to the theme of the lesson, for instance sports.

Example:
My name is Julie, and I like baseball.

NAME GAME: MY NAME IS . . . . Going around the circle, players state their first and last names. Then, using either one, each player states something that he or she likes or dislikes about the name.

Examples:
My name is Felicity Johnson. I like Felicity because it is my grandmother's name, and I like being named after her.
My name is Joe Fox. I dislike Fox because people ask me if I'm sly.

Older groups enjoy thinking about their names. They frequently have enough life experience to relate their likes and dislikes to such things as family history and school memories. In listening to the likes and dislikes of classmates, participants will sometimes laugh or smile as they relate others' responses to their own frames of reference. By associating the comment with the player offering it, participants are making connections that will help them remember the speaker's name.

NAME GAME: I'M GOING TO THE ZOO AND I'M GOING TO SEE .... This activity is a variation of a letter-matching name game. It accomplishes two objectives: getting acquainted and developing concentration. Going around the circle, players state their names, each one mentioning something he or she would see at the zoo that begins with the same letter as his or her first name. Players repeat items already named before adding their own.

Example:

Player 1: I'm Amy. I'm going to the zoo, and I'm going to see an alligator.

Player 2: I'm Larry. I'm going to the zoo, and I'm going to see an alligator and a lion.

Player 3: I'm Yolonda. I'm going to the zoo, and I'm going to see an alligator, a lion, and a yak.

Player 4: I'm Zach. I'm going to the zoo, and I'm going to see an alligator, a lion, a yak, and the zookeeper.

Leaders can think of many variations that can be thematically related or personalized. A scout troop, for example, may wish to go to camp. Leaders can use states and their capitals ("I'm going to Texas to visit the capital [Austin]"), or countries, continents, and other places (glaciers, mountains, etc.), for integrating geography. For science integration, players can travel to planets and imagine what they will see!

Sometimes players can be too enthusiastic, responding when it isn't their turn. There is a fine line, however, between being supportive (aiding memory) and stifling response. The leader should encourage players to help one another when assistance is truly necessary.

NAME GAME: THE INTERVIEW. The interview activity involves pairing the players and giving them time to talk together. If desired, they can jot down pertinent information. Next, each player introduces the partner to the class, stating the name and additional information about the person that has been learned during the interview. This helps in remembering names and encourages careful listening. It is appropriate for older groups where the players do not know each other well.

NAME GAME: THE INTERVIEW, VARIATION 1. Rather than straightforward introductions, players can create radio and television commercials extolling the virtues of the partners they have just interviewed. Younger players can create short spots, as in the example below.

Example:

This is Alison. She is unique because she's lived in New Zealand. No class should be without her. Every class should have its own world traveler. Call 1-800-ZEA-LAND to make Alison ours!

Older players' commercials should last thirty to sixty seconds.

NAME GAME: THE INTERVIEW, VARIATION 2. Each player converts the information gained during the interview into new lyrics and then sings the introduction to a familiar tune.

Example:
(to the tune of "Mary Had a Little Lamb")
Alison's from New Zealand, New Zealand, New Zealand.
She likes drama and reading books.
She's going to be my friend.

NAME GAME: BODY LETTERS. In this activity, players show their names by spelling the letters with their bodies. A player can form all of the letters or can ask other players to assist. Body Letters, in fact, works especially well in small groups; together, all members of the group form each player's name.

NAME GAME: INITIALS. For some players, spelling entire names with their bodies may be too difficult, and forming only initials is a better choice. In this activity, forming either upper- or lower-case letters is acceptable and provides an obvious link to language arts.

To play, the group is divided in half. One at a time, players in the first group form the initial of their first or last names. Members of the other group watch; and when someone recognizes a letter, that person correctly identifies the player and the initial. A match forms a partnership and is useful for pairing players for later activities. This game is recommended when players do not know each other well.

NAME GAME: LET YOUR HANDS DO THE TALKING. This game sharpens listening skills and expands rhythmic skills. It is effective when players know one another's names. Going around the circle, players individually say their names and then clap the rhythms of their names. For example, Timothy will first say "Timothy" and then clap three times while saying his name again. The players then echo his name, and echo it again while clapping the rhythm.

Example:
First player: (recite)
Tim-o-thy
(clap)   X X X
All players: (recite)
Tim-o-thy

(recite and clap)
Tim-o-thy
X   X   X
Next player: (recite)
Da-nis-ta Lu
(clap)   X X X X
All players: (recite)
Da-nis-ta Lu
(recite and clap)
Da-nis-ta Lu
X   X   X   X

After everyone has had a turn, it might be fun to just clap names and play an identification game. The leader, for instance, will ask all players to stand whose names "sound" like this: *clap, clap*.

NAME GAME: LET YOUR HANDS DO THE TALKING VARIATION. Instead of using hand clapping, the players take turns using a drum to express their names. Players should note how loudly or softly names are performed. The drum might be explored for gentle swishing, scratching, tapping, and traditional striking sounds.

NAME GAME: NAMES ARE FINE—DO YOU KNOW MINE? The leader recites the following chant until the players can recite it alone:

Names, names, names are *fine.*
You say *yours* and *I'll* say *mine.*

While rehearsing the chant, a **patchen** (thigh-slap) keeps the beat steady during recitation. (The italicized words receive the patchen beat.) Players recite the chant in unison while keeping a steady beat with the patchen. Then players take turns saying their names; the group repeats, allowing one free beat between names. The group repeats the chant again, and a second player continues. After every player has had a turn, the chant becomes twice as fast and changes to

Names, names, names are *fine.*
Time to *test*, do *you* know *mine*?

To conclude, the group then recites each player's name while maintaining the beat. If the momentum is interrupted (as players' names might be forgotten), the chant begins again.

FINGER PLAYS (LOWER LEVEL)

Finger plays are short poems, chants, or rhythmic activities that encourage active listening and participation on a limited scale. For preschool or lower elementary players, they are simple, structured, and enjoyable early excursions into creative drama and movement. Older players, however, will find the verses unsuited to their maturity level.

Finger plays use repetition to help build players' confidence. The leader should model actions and words before inviting them to join. Once all know the poem, it is played in unison.

Finger plays can be performed anywhere and can be used between routine classroom activities for a change of pace: at the beginning of a session to focus attention or to prepare players for more vigorous activity. Depending on the verse, they can be used to teach body parts (health), numbers (math), or animals (science), or they can appeal to a player's imagination, sense of humor, or need to move. Once accustomed to doing finger plays, players can go from imitation to more imaginative involvement by creating their own verses and actions.

"Hands and Feet"
Clap your hands,
(clap hands)
Clap your hands,
(clap hands)
Wave them all around.
(wave hands)

Stamp your feet,
(stamp feet)
Stamp your feet,
(stamp feet)
Really shake the ground.
(stamp several times)

"See My Nose"
See my nose
(point to nose)
On my face.
(place hand on face)
What a perfect
(cup hands in sleeping gesture)
Resting place.
See my eyes
(point to eyes)
Open wide.
(make circles with fingers and place in front of eyes)
From them nothing
(cover eyes with fingers, leaving open spaces between fingers)
Much can hide.
See my finger
(place finger on lips)
On my lips.
From that quiet
(make hushing sound)
Nothing slips.

"Tall/Small"
I can stand up so tall,
(stand on tiptoe)
See above the highest wall.
(hand above eyes in looking gesture)
I can curl up so small,
(curl up in ball)
You won't think I'm there at all!
(become as small as possible)

NURSERY RHYME FINGER PLAYS (LOWER LEVEL)

Many familiar nursery rhymes can be adapted to finger plays by the leader and players. The latter find this interpretive freedom particularly enjoyable. The finger and hand motions usually illustrate the meanings of words, but the creative process allows players to illustrate feelings, rhythmic expression, motions, or even abstractions.

As an example, "Hickory, Dickory, Dock" is a familiar rhyme whose words may suggest particular movement ideas:

Hickory, dickory, dock,
(hand imitates pendulum swing)
The mouse ran up the clock.
(fingers walk upward)
The clock struck one,
(clap once, indicate "one" with index finger)
The mouse ran down,
(fingers walk downward)
Hickory, dickory, dock.
(hand imitates pendulum swing)

The literal performance of nursery rhymes is suggested before moving to creative interpretations. For example, after discussing movements of different types of clocks, movements of a little mouse, and the difference between up and down, players can "choreograph" their own finger play movements to express the feelings, the speed of the action, or their individual interpretations of the nursery rhyme. For additional enjoyment, players can join in singing the rhyme with the finger play. The sequence of experience is for players first to design finger plays illustrating literal interpretation of rhymes and then eventually to choreograph their own creative plays.

There are many books that inventory rhymes and chants, but few address how they might be conveyed to young people. It is, therefore, up to the leader to adapt these wonderful materials. A few more examples illustrate the rich potential for creative expressiveness in finger plays.

"Pat-a-Cake"
Pat-a-cake, pat-a-cake, baker's man,
Bake me a cake as fast as you can;
Pat it and prick it, and mark it with a *B*,
Put it in the oven for baby and me.

"Hey Diddle Diddle"
Hey diddle diddle,
The cat and the fiddle,
The cow jumped over the moon;
The little dog laughed
To see such sport,
And the dish ran away with the spoon.

"Little Boy Blue"
Little boy blue,
Come blow your horn.
The sheep's in the meadow,
The cow's in the corn.
Where is the boy who looks after the sheep?
He's under a haystack fast asleep.
Will you wake him?
No, not I.
For if I do he's sure to cry.

To help players move creatively during finger plays, the rhythmic flow and lilt of each nursery rhyme need to be stressed. Such emphasis gives rise to sensing musical elements such as the **beat**, **rhythm**, and **accents**. This will help them perform with more artistic expression. The following rhyme serves as an example:

"Twinkle, Twinkle, Little Star"
Twinkle, twinkle, little star,
How I wonder what you are!
Up above the world so high,
Like a diamond in the sky.
Twinkle, twinkle, little star,
How I wonder what you are.

To feel the rhythmical flow of the chant, players can toe tap. They should feel four beats and some accents in each line of the rhyme. (The accents occur on the italicized syllables or words in the following verses.) To help reinforce the beat, the leader can couple movements with syllables:

Twinkle, twinkle, little star,
(open and close fist four times)
How I wonder what you are!
(with hands open, shrug four times)
Up above the world so high,
(hands "climb" four steps high)
Like a diamond in the sky.
(trace four sides of diamond shape)
Twinkle, twinkle, little star,
(open and close fist four times)
How I wonder what you are.
(with hands open, shrug four times)

Following a unison performance, a more creative activity allows players to express the meaning of the rhyme through original movements that match their feelings. For example, the leader might ask the players to experiment with a "twinkle" on their faces and in their hands, or to imagine looking at a twinkling sky. "What kind of a sky do we have? A bright, sunny day sky? A cold, cloudy night sky?" The objective of such interpretation is far different from that of unison performance on rhythmic beats. In unison activities, players synchronize movements together with little room for creative (individual) interpretation. A more experimental activity allows the players to use their imaginations, expressing individual thoughts and feelings. The structured unison and unstructured interpretations accomplish two different results.

NOISY STORIES
(LOWER/UPPER LEVELS)

In a **noisy story**, players participate by making sounds assigned to characters. Each major character is assigned a sound or phrase. Each time that character is mentioned in the story, the players utter that sound or phrase. This is one of the most delightful activities used in creative drama. It works equally well with younger and older players, although the presentation of the story, the subject matter, and the difficulty level of the material will vary somewhat depending upon the age of the participants.

Several advantages are associated with the use of noisy stories:

- They involve the entire group and, as a beginning activity, remove attention from the individual.
- For younger players, characters and sounds can be developed to help instruct the proper formation of vowel and consonant sounds.
- Players can be encouraged to participate loudly and constructively channel excess energy.
- These stories encourage players to listen closely so that they can make their sounds on cue.
- Noisy stories encourage expressive vocal delivery.
- Noisy stories that the players particularly enjoy can be set aside and saved for later use as stories to dramatize.

The most common procedure for leading a noisy story is to put the players in groups and assign each group a character. When the group is small or the players very young, however, it is wiser to select a story with only a few characters and allow the entire group to do each one in unison. This helps those who tend to feel inhibited or who forget easily. In either case, it is helpful for the leader to make the sounds with the players or to cue each group visually. Knowing the story well enough to maintain eye contact with the players ensures success.

In selecting, writing, or adapting a noisy story, it is better to have only a few characters who appear frequently than it is to have many who appear only once. It is also important to scramble the order, for if characters always appear in a consistent sequence, the players will listen only for the character that comes before their own. They will anticipate cues rather than listening carefully to the story.

To prepare the presentation, the leader should score the paper, writing character names in capital letters, placing asterisks or dots after the names, or in some other way setting them off as a reminder to stop for the sounds. Forgetting often brings a loud protest from the group. In some cases, it might be useful to tell the story once before assigning sounds, to familiarize players with the plot.

It is best to assign a character and sound to a group, demonstrate the character's sound, and have the players practice that sound several times. This allows the leader to check for comprehension and to encourage those who may be shy or hesitant.

Stories children are reading can be easily adapted into noisy stories. The leader should select a story that has several interesting characters and create sounds for them. The activity is played as previously described.

The following noisy stories attest to the versatility of the form.

Noisy Story: "The Big Race"

Mark: "va va va vroom"	Jenny: "chug chug"
Alan: "thump thump"	Patty: "pull pull"

Mark,* Alan,* Jenny,* and Patty* had been working hard to get ready for the big race. Mark* had spent all week working on his bike, a bright red model with training wheels. Mark* had painted the bike and decorated it with streamers. When he rode it, Mark* felt like he was flying. Alan* had practiced

all week on his pogo stick and could bounce for blocks without losing his balance. Jenny* and her sister, Patty,* had converted Jenny's* wagon into a train by adding a cardboard smokestack to the front. Whenever Patty* pulled the wagon, Jenny* sat inside it and imagined great white puffs of smoke rising from the cardboard cylinder. Jenny* pretended to be an engineer.

On Saturday morning, Mark,* Alan,* Jenny,* and Patty* met at the top of Maple Street. Patty* took a piece of chalk from her pocket and drew a line across the sidewalk. "This is the starting line," said Patty.* Mark,* Alan,* and Jenny* moved into position behind the line and checked their vehicles. Then Patty* walked down the street and drew another line across the sidewalk, several blocks from the starting position. "This is the finish line," said Patty.* "Whoever crosses it first wins." Then Patty* ran back to Jenny's* wagon, picked up the handle, and said, "One, two, three, go!"

Mark,* Alan,* Jenny,* and Patty* took off down the sidewalk. Jenny* and Patty* quickly passed Alan* and Mark.* Before long, however, Mark* pedaled past the other children. He rode his bike across the finish line and yelled with glee, "I won!" Alan,* Jenny,* and Patty* congratulated Mark.* All four friends agreed that the race had been great fun and looked forward to another contest next Saturday.

Noisy stories offer an enjoyable format for teaching or checking articulation skills. In the preceding story, for example, *v* is a *labiodental* sound (made with lips and teeth), *th* is a dental sound, *ch* is an *affricative* (made by audible friction as the stop consonant is released), and *p* is a *bilabial* sound (made with two lips).

In "The Big Race," all characters appear for a final time at the end of the story. While this is optional, it allows the players one last opportunity to make their sounds.

Noisy Story: "The Legend of Lightning Man"

Many cultures have stories that explain natural phenomena. The following noisy story has been inspired by several legends but is, in fact, an original creation designed to show the leader how such material might be adapted. Folk tales such as this one fit well into social studies, multicultural education, and language arts lessons.

Lightning Man: Sky: "look up"
   "crash, zap, crackle" Stones: "plunk,
Sister: "good joke"   kerplunk"
River: "ebb and flow"

Long, long ago, Lightning Man* did not live in the sky.* Lightning Man* lived beneath a river.* Sister* lived there, too. Lightning Man* often would emerge from the river* and walk the lands looking for game and other food. Sister* would also walk the land, looking for fruits and insects to eat.

One day, when Lightning Man* went out hunting, Sister* stayed behind. Sister* decided to play a trick on Lightning Man.* Sister* came out of the river* and onto the land. Sister* hid near the shore.

Soon, Lightning Man* returned from hunting and moved into his home beneath the river.* Sister* began to throw stones* into the river.* Sister* knew that Lightning Man* did not like to be disturbed. Sister* thought it would be great fun to tease Lightning Man* by throwing stones* into the river.*

Lightning Man* came angrily out of the river* as the stones* made ripple after ripple. Lightning Man* did not like Sister's* joke. In a rage, Lightning Man* yelled and screamed at Sister.* Lightning Man* found Sister* on the shore

and chased her. Sister* was frightened and tried to run, but Lightning Man* caught Sister.*

The guardian spirits had been watching and decided to end the fight between Lightning Man* and Sister.* They whisked Lightning Man* into the sky* and turned Sister* into several large stones.* Sister,* in the form of stones,* still resides by the river,* and Lightning Man* still lives in the sky.*

Noisy Story: "Mary Anderson, Inventor"

Older players will be intrigued by the story of Mary Anderson. This woman's contribution to transportation safety can enhance science lessons about inventors and inventions, and it illustrates the important ground work one woman laid with her innovative thinking. Perhaps players will remember this story the next time they are riding in a vehicle in the rain.

Mary Anderson: Streetcar:
   "I'm an inventor!"   "clang, clang"
Windshield Wiper: Doubters:
   "swish, swoosh"   "It will
                                   never work"

In 1903, women were expected to be housewives, not inventors. Mary Anderson,* however, was not a typical Southern belle. Born in Alabama, Mary Anderson* traveled to New York City and often rode on a streetcar.* Mary Anderson* noticed that the streetcar* driver had to get out of his seat to clean the streetcar's window, even if the weather was fair. When it rained or snowed, the streetcar* driver had to clean the window more often. Mary Anderson* thought that this was dangerous.

Mary Anderson made many early designs for her invention, the windshield wiper.* She worked on designing a windshield wiper* that was manually operated from inside the streetcar.* When the streetcar* driver pulled the lever, the windshield wiper* arm moved over the windshield.* When Mary Anderson* completed her design, the windshield wiper* blade had rubber on it and was attached to a spring-loaded arm. Pulling the lever made the windshield wiper* blade glide across the glass before returning to its original position.

Doubters,* however, scoffed at Mary Anderson's idea. The doubters* claimed that the windshield wiper* would distract drivers. The doubters* could not see that the windshield wiper* could benefit all drivers, not just streetcar* operators. The doubters* said that the windshield wiper* would cause accidents. The doubters* thought that the windshield wiper* would only be useful in winter, if at all.

Mary Anderson* proved the doubters* wrong. In 1905, Mary Anderson* received a patent for her windshield wiper.* Today, there are no doubters.* All vehicle drivers, as well as passengers, know that Mary Anderson's* invention made travel safer.

As a follow-up science activity, players could research another inventor and invention. They could then write a noisy story based upon their investigation.

Noisy Story, Noiseless Variation:
"Unhappy Hank Finds Friends"
In the noiseless variation, rather than using sounds or words, the leader assigns each character a facial expression. Players are told what to do, but not how to do it. This variation can be used in preparing the players for pantomime, when noise is undesirable, or when teaching abstract concepts such as emotions. When the character is named, players respond through facial expression.

Sweet Sue: smiling, happy face
Brave Bart: brave face
Unhappy Hank: sad face
Mean Mike: mean face

Unhappy Hank* was unhappy because he thought no one liked him. Unhappy Hank* wanted very much to be popular. Mean Mike* knew that Unhappy Hank* wanted a friend and thought of a mean plan. Mean Mike* told Unhappy Hank* that he would be his friend if Unhappy Hank* would help him steal Brave Bart's* horse. Unhappy Hank* knew it was wrong to steal, but he wanted Mean Mike* to be his friend and agreed to help.

Sweet Sue* was eating dinner with Brave Bart* at Brave Bart's* house when they heard a noise coming from the barn. Sweet Sue* and Brave Bart* went out to the barn to look. There they saw Unhappy Hank* and Mean Mike* trying to lead Brave Bart's* horse out of the barn. Brave Bart* yelled, "Stop, thieves!" Mean Mike* tried to run away, but Sweet Sue* tripped him before he could reach the door.

Unhappy Hank* started to cry. Unhappy Hank* said, "I'm sorry. I didn't want to steal Brave Bart's* horse. I just wanted Mean Mike* to like me. I wanted a friend." Brave Bart* reassured Unhappy Hank,* "Don't worry. We like you. We'll be your friends." Sweet Sue* said, "After the sheriff comes for Mean Mike,* Brave Bart* and I want you to join us for dinner." Unhappy Hank* knew he had found real friends at last, and he smiled.

REPLAYING (LOWER/UPPER LEVELS)

After the players have finished an activity, it may be desirable to **replay** it. In creative drama, replaying or playing an activity again, should always have a positive rather than a negative connotation. Activities are not replayed because they are done incorrectly, but because playing will improve with repetition. Replay should be incorporated into a session when it will improve play, give new players a chance to participate, or bring new interpretations to the activity. The process is both constructive and exploratory. Often a story will be done more enthusiastically a second time, as players become more familiar and comfortable with material. In a replay, the activity can be made more challenging. The leader, for example, might ask the children to stand as they make their sounds.

Replaying should be considered when interest merits it and its use will bring positive changes. Activities in this chapter, and throughout this book, can be replayed to enhance creative drama experiences. In noisy stories, for example, one group might determine that they should respond more in unison. Later, in more advanced activities such as story creation and story dramatization, players might, for example, want to try different interpretations of a character. Regardless of the type of activity, replay can be a valuable tool for guiding players.

Notice how the leader might facilitate a replay of "The Big Race."

Replay: "The Big Race"

Leader: Now that we've played the story once and know our character and sound well, let's replay. This time, when your character is mentioned in the story, stand to make your sound, and sit immediately afterward. What else might we do?

Player: We could be louder and clearer.

Leader: Good suggestion. Let's also see if we can project our voices clearly this time.

Mark* (players stand), Alan* (players stand), Jenny* (players stand), and

Patty* (players stand) had been working hard to get ready for the big race . . .

As the replay continues, the leader should notice that the players' responses are louder and clearer.

SOUND AWARENESS

Listening Levels

Listening skills are integral to success in learning. For example, if children have problems listening, they will experience difficulties in all content areas, since many lessons involve attention to aural information.

With young players, one should not assume that they are listening to the beat of the same drummer. In fact, they may not be listening at all! The leader will have to strengthen the players' listening skills before optimal creative work can be accomplished. In advanced creative drama and music activities, keen listening skills are even more important. The skillful leader needs to devise activities that develop players' skills from marginal to analytical in interesting and challenging contexts.

There are three levels of listening, and leaders can develop players' listening skills through a variety of enjoyable activities. These levels are **marginal**, **attentive**, and **analytical** listening.

Marginal listeners hear all sounds in the environment and give equal aural value to them. Thus, while listening to directions to an activity, if another player sneezes, or if traffic noise occurs, the marginal listener hears all of these sounds as equally important. Many young players are at the marginal level in listening skill development.

Attentive listeners can give some aural priority to a single sound source. For example, they can pay attention to spoken directions over other sounds. This ability to focus and concentrate on one sound source needs deliberate practice and reinforcement for most young players. Specific music activities can sharpen marginal listeners into becoming attentive listeners.

Analytical listeners not only focus on a single sound source, but they can describe characteristics. For example, in listening to spoken directions, they will be able to determine if the person's voice is high or low. The ability to analyze sounds requires continuous development. The activities that follow, involving sound awareness, found sounds, body sounds, and instrumental sounds, help players refine listening skills creatively.

Sound Scavenger Hunt (Lower/Upper Levels)

Building upon the familiar hunt for objects, this activity asks players to search for sounds and listen carefully. Players will engage in active listening that requires focus and analysis.

SCAVENGER HUNT GAME: WHAT CAN YOU FIND? In this activity, players (usually in pairs or small groups) explore the environment and record interesting sounds that they hear. Their collection of sounds can be played back for other players to hear and enjoy.

SCAVENGER HUNT GAME: CAN YOU FIND SPECIFIC SOUNDS? Another variation is for players to collect a specific list of sounds, such as traffic noises, animal sounds, machine sounds, kitchen sounds, cartoon characters, friends' voices, or weather sounds. Reminding players that it is a good idea to keep a checklist of all sounds recorded will minimize their forgetfulness.

SCAVENGER HUNT GAME: WHAT DO YOU HEAR? In this activity, the players first listen to others' recordings of sounds and

try to identify them. The players then try to imitate the sounds using their voices, movements, or instruments.

Found Sound (Lower/Upper Levels)

Found sound games, which are logical extensions of scavenger hunts, refine listening skills further. Found sounds are noises that players can manipulate using materials, objects, or equipment in the natural environment. Where can found sounds be found? Pencils scraped along spirals of notebooks, keys or coins jingled, trash cans tapped, ball-point pens clicked, and three-ring binders opened and closed represent a small sample of the sound sources that can be found within most classrooms. Sample objects for making found sounds are listed at the end of this chapter.

Found sound activities provide an opportunity for players to show how resourceful they can be in discovering and manipulating different noises. As with scavenger hunt activities, players will become attentive in their listening to found sounds. To sharpen listening skills, noises can be recorded and analyzed.

Leaders can help players realize that found sound activities are deliberate and purposeful. Random banging on objects for willy-nilly effect is not the point. Noises for found sound do not need to be loud to be interesting. Players should be encouraged to discover subtleties of different sounds and to manipulate ordinary objects for eerie, funny, beautiful, and surprising effects.

In addition to refining listening skills, the following activities stretch the imagination. They begin with simple experimentation with available sounds and lead to challenging compositions. The young player needs a fair amount of experience to develop sharp listening skills.

The leader is wise to spend a little time drawing attention to the fine distinctions between various sounds, so that the players may use them selectively in future activities.

Is found sound music? How are found sound compositions considered "musical"? In musical compositions, the elements are deliberately managed. The rhythm is precise, not random. The **tempo** is determined and controlled. The exact **pitch** levels (high or low tones) are chosen. The **dynamics** (degrees of loudness or softness) are carefully manipulated. In found sound compositions, these elements are organized the same way—just as a composer manipulates sound ideas for a musical composition.

FOUND SOUND ACTIVITY: RAINSTORM SOUND STORY. In groups of three or four, players plan a sixty-second found sound piece to tell the story of a rainstorm. One player is designated the "conductor," for leading the final performance. The players will need to plan how the storm begins, what sounds will be used for rain (or thunder, wind, splashing, etc.), and how to follow the direction of the storm. The overall **form** of the sound piece needs to be planned. For example, the players may plan a gentle **overture** to the storm, an active middle, and a gradual, tapering end to the sound story.

After the leader allows each group to rehearse its rainstorm, it is performed for other groups. Players give their compositions titles, and the conductors introduce them. After performances, they critique the sound stories, discussing which sounds were particularly effective in conveying the elements of the storm.

More advanced students demonstrate their understanding of the elements of weather (science) by exploring different types of storms through found sound compositions, such as tornadoes, hurricanes, typhoons, tsunamis, and sandstorms The fine distinctions should be made obvious through carefully selected found sounds, skillful performance of musical elements, and creative titles.

FOUND SOUND ACTIVITY: GROUP POPCORN. As a large group activity, players plan a one-minute found sound composition entitled "Poppa Corn Gets Popped." They plan the order in which the events happen when popcorn is made. Then they determine if it will be made in a microwave oven, on the stove top, over an open camp fire, or in a special popcorn maker. Within the environment, they explore sounds to represent each event. After some experimentation, they select the sounds that are best for telling the story. A designated conductor should lead the movement of sounds, because no talking is permitted during the sound story.

As an extension of the activity, the group may then practice the composition and perform it for recording. Later, make a recording of the sounds of actual corn being popped and compare and contrast the two.

FOUND SOUND ACTIVITY: ALMOST LATE FOR THE BUS. This activity challenges players to think about the form (organization) of a musical piece. In small groups, upper-level players plan a three- to four-minute sound piece that begins with the door closing (leaving the house) and ends with the bus door closing. They plan for one character to walk leisurely to the bus stop and find sounds to tell the story of what is seen and heard. Toward the end of the walk, the character realizes the bus has already arrived and hurries not to be late. Groups may then record the found sounds for analysis.

FOUND SOUND ACTIVITY: FOUND SOUND POETRY. The leader prepares for this activity by selecting a poem to perform using found sounds in the environment. For example, "Bath Time" is a poem that lends itself to interesting rhythms and suggests expressive sounds.

"Bath Time"
Sliberdy, sluberdy,
Glub a dub dub.
Sliberdy, sloshity,
Suds in the tub.
Sliberdy, sluberdy,
Bath toys come in.
Scrubity, dubity,
Glistening skin.
Sliberdy, sluberdy,
Soap in my eye.
Dripity, drybity,
Now I won't cry!

The players will want to find sounds to represent the "sliberdy," "sluberdy," and "sloshity" sounds. If the activity is to be experienced with very young players, combine the found sounds with a leader's reading of the poem. Older players may wish to read the poem out loud with found sounds accompanying it. A more interesting version is to perform the poem substituting found sounds for the spoken words "sliberdy," "sluberdy," and "sloshity."

There are books that are ideal for creating found sound poetry. Works by Dr. Seuss and Maurice Sendak, for example, are wonderful resources for this activity.

FOUND SOUND ACTIVITY: OPEN-ENDED SOUND STORY. This baseball story is appropriate for a large group. Players find sounds to orchestrate a ninth inning with the bases loaded. First, they discuss what could happen in the inning. They recognize that fly balls, strikes, foul balls, hits, and home runs, for example, will all have different sounds. They find objects and explore different qualities of sound effects.

Next, the group is divided into smaller groups of five or six players. Each small group may plan its own ninth inning and perform it for the entire group. Listeners are asked to determine what happened in each scenario based on the found sounds.

EXPANDING THE ORCHESTRA OF FOUND SOUNDS. Found sound activities may be expanded by players using additional sound sources from home. Imagine the variety of "instruments" that could be used from the home office, kitchen, or garage.

Players improve their listening skills through found sound activities, and they also enjoy the discovery and expression of special sound characteristics that can be found in common, ordinary items within their classrooms or homes. These activities lay the foundation for creative **composition**, using other (traditional and nontraditional) sound media.

A number of contemporary composers have used found sounds in clever ways in their compositions. Keyboards, train whistles, and cannons are but a few interesting sound effects. The twentieth-century American composer Henry Partsch used brake drums for beautiful found sounds in his works.

Body Sounds (Lower/Upper Levels)
Body sounds can complement found sounds effectively and widen the palette for a creative orchestra. Like found sounds, body sounds are an effective way to creatively accompany events. Examples of body sounds include clapping, stomping, snapping fingers, patchen, bopping hands (fist on top of fist), rubbing hands together, shuffling feet, and mouth sounds such as finger pops, hissing, tongue clucking, humming, buzzing, blowing, or even "tsk-tsking"!

Hand jives are one class of body sounds. These involve a set of two to

Table 2.1. Found Sound Sources

Kitchen instruments	Sewing supply instruments	Garage instruments	Miscellaneous instruments
aerosol can tops	beads	brushes	balloons
cans	buttons	clamps	balls
dry beans, rice, peas in small jars	elastic strips	gardening tools	bubble wrap
egg beater	measuring tape	hammers	cellophane
funnel	safety pins	hand tools	clothespins
grater	scissors	hangers	corrugated cardboard
measuring cups	snaps	hoses	newspaper
metal cutlery	spools of thread	inner tubes	sandpaper
oatmeal boxes	yardstick/ruler	nails	shoes
paper cups	zippers	oil can	spiral notebook
pie plates		pipes	springs
plastic cutlery		potting supplies	tin foil
pot and pan lids		trash cans	tissue paper
rubber bands		watering can	toys
soda pop bottles			wax paper
straws			whistles
toaster			
tongs			
whisks			
wooden spoons			

four movements made by the hands (and arms) to form a pattern that is repeated. For example, a player may create a hand jive alternating thigh slapping and hand clapping. Each sound has its own characteristic quality.

Vocal sounds are another class of body sounds. Players innately and sometimes unconsciously vocalize during their play. They are quite inventive in generating sounds to imitate the environment. For example, many can mimic computer games quite accurately. The voice is a wondrous instrument in itself and can be manipulated for an infinite number of effects.

The following activities begin to demonstrate some spontaneous, creative expressions using body sounds. They also will require players to listen carefully and reinforce musical concepts.

BODY SOUND ACTIVITY: VOICING A STORY WITHOUT WORDS. One natural starting point for body sound activity is to transfer a found sound composition to body sounds. To illustrate, after the found sound game of "Poppa Corn Gets Popped," the leader asks players to use only vocal sounds to perform it. Other clever compositions might be entitled "A Visit to the Zoo," "The Green Tornado," or "Demolition Derby in Slow Motion." The leader invites players to explore the sound characteristics of pitch level and dynamics to build interest in the sound story. Players discover the richness of using lips, teeth, and tongue for special effects.

BODY/FOUND/INSTRUMENT ACTIVITY: STORY FOR FULL ORCHESTRA. Players might enjoy combining classroom instruments with found sounds and body sounds into a single creative piece. Simple instruments, in partnership with body and found sounds, will contribute to the sound potential of story orchestration. These might include triangles, bells, tone blocks, tambourines, and resonator bells (or xylophones). In collaboration with a creative drama activity, the full orchestra can be used for "stand alone" music pieces such as an overture (an introduction to a work) or an **interlude**

(music between acts or between scenes), or it can take an **accompaniment** role as background to a story (language arts).

BODY SOUND ACTIVITY: BODY SOUND ACCOMPANIMENT. Body sounds can accompany singing or movement experiences in natural yet special ways. Using the example of "Take Me Out to the Ballgame," players supply appropriate body sounds through a repeated pattern, such as *patchen* (pat thigh), *clap, clap.* This three-movement pattern forms a hand jive and accompanies the entire song with a steady beat. (Note: A sequence of three movements fits the tune because it has a triple meter, i.e., an "um, pah, pah" or waltz feeling.)

The number of movements in the hand jive pattern corresponds to the meter of the song. It is helpful if the leader identifies the meter accurately. If the hand jive is wrong, it will feel awkward when performed with the song.

Most chants or songs are felt in **duple** (two) or **triple** (three) beat patterns. "Yankee Doodle," for example, has a duple meter, and the hand jive should have two movements in it. "Chim Chim Cher-ee" has triple meter, and the pattern should have three movements. Though some hand jives may use two or three distinct movements, these movement patterns should be repeated throughout the song. To make the hand jive interesting for older players, two patterns may be alternated (see illustrations that follow). Care should be taken, however, to

X = one beat and each measure will contain four counts.

clap		X		X	│		X	X	X	‖
patchen	X		X		│	X				

Using notation where ♩ = one beat, the hand jive can be read as follows:

Figure 2.1

Figure 2.2

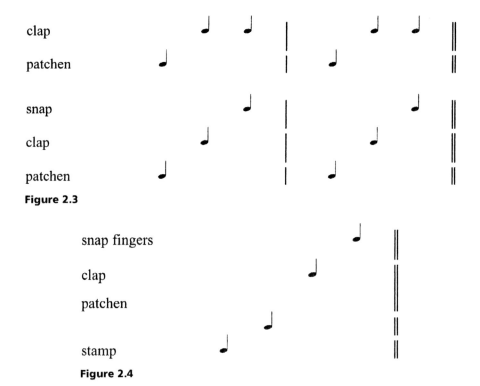

clap

patchen

snap

clap

patchen

Figure 2.3

snap fingers

clap

patchen

stamp

Figure 2.4

avoid too many different movements that become frustrating to perform naturally with the tempo.

Hand jives can be created for varying skill levels. Leaders know the fine motor development of their players. While young players may not be able to snap fingers, they can tap their index fingers together for a creative motion. Advanced players will appreciate more complicated patterns.

All sorts of clever patterns for hand jives can be invented. As players progress, these patterns of sounds can be choreographed to enhance chanting, stories, singing, or movement activities. It is a good idea to practice the pattern several times before adding the song or chant.

Figure 2.1 shows some simple hand jives that can be used with duple-meter songs or chants (two- or four-beat patterns).

Upper-level players may work with a specific partner, or the leader may prefer to have any number of students sit in a circle to perform partner hand jives with their adjacent neighbors. Figure 2.2 shows partner/neighbor hand jives.

Figure 2.3 shows some warm-ups that can be used with songs or chants having three-beat patterns (and three beats per measure).

More advanced hand jives, as shown in figure 2.4, challenge upper-level players' coordination beyond hands.

A list of familiar songs suitable for hand-jive accompaniment can be found at the end of this chapter.

BODY SOUND ACTIVITY: HAND JIVES FOR RECORDED MUSIC. Introducing hand jives through recorded music frees the leader to demonstrate the pattern. This also allows players to focus on one task: coordinating the movements with the **meter** of the music. The leader prepares by selecting a recorded tune that players know. Then

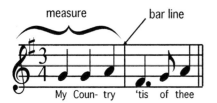

Figure 2.5

Reading Rhythm

Not every classroom teacher can read music. Separating rhythmic reading from melodic reading makes the task simpler. Through simple activities and basic notation, leaders can acquire the skills to lead rhythmic activities confidently. The reading skills that follow will guide leaders step by step to assist in music reading.

Rhythm is musical time. When experiencing rhythm, notice the beat (steady pulse); tempo (speed of beats); length of notes (**duration**); and meter (groupings of beats). Some beats are slightly

Name	Note	Rest
Whole Note	𝅝	
Half Note	𝅗𝅥	
Quarter Note	♩	
Eighth Note	♪	
Sixteenth Note	♬	

Figure 2.6

(♩)

Figure 2.7

emphasized (accented). All of these aspects of musical time make rhythm interesting to experience. Give players ample experience listening and responding to rhythm before asking them to analyze it.

The leader who uses printed music will find this preview helpful. Musical notation is ruled off by vertical lines forming **measures** or **bars**. At the start of the music is a set of numbers that convey how many beats are grouped into each measure and what the note value is for each beat. These numerical notations are known as **time signature** or **meter signature**. The numerator will reveal the meter. The denominator indicates the beat value, that is, the type of note receiving one count in each measure.

For example, in the song "America" (figure 2.5), the time signature's top number (*3*) reveals that there will be three beats in each measure.

If the top number is a *2* or a *4*, the music is felt as duple meter. Duple meter means the beats are felt in sets of two, as in a marching pattern. If the numerator is a *3*, as in "America" (figure 2.5), the music is felt as a triple meter. Triple meter means beats are felt in sets of three, as in a waltz pattern. A *6* in the numerator usually will be felt as duple meter (two rapid sets of three beats). Most chants, rhymes, songs, or musical compositions can be felt as duple meter or triple meter.

Figure 2.6 is a chart that illustrates the common note and rest symbols in youth music.[1]

In the illustration of the time signature in "America," the bottom number (*4*) indicates that the quarter note (figure 2.7) is the beat value. If the bottom number of the time signature is a *2*, the half note

the leader asks them to listen and identify the beat by tapping their toes. Once the beat is felt, the meter may be discovered by sensing where accents occur.

Hush, lit-tle ba - by, don't say a word, ma-ma's gon-na buy you a mock-ikng-bird.

Figure 2.8

receives one count and is the beat value. In most songs, the bottom number is a *4*, indicating that a quarter note receives one beat. An *8* in the denominator, however, would indicate that the eighth note is the beat value.

The most common time signature is 4/4 time. It is so common that composers might place a "C" on the staff as shorthand for the "common time" of 4/4. In this signature, there are four beats in each measure, and the quarter note receives one count. This is **quadruple meter**.

A list of familiar songs is included in this chapter. And leaders can determine if they are duple or triple meter by performing them and sensing the meter. Check your understanding of reading rhythm by reviewing the rhythm to the familiar song, "The Mocking Bird." (See Figure 2.8.) How many beats are in each measure? What is the meter? What type of note gets one beat? What types get more or less than a beat? Can you keep a steady beat (X) by tapping your toe and clapping the rhythm of the song?

FAMILIAR SONGS

The Alley, Alley Oh
America
Are You Sleeping?
The Barnyard Song
The Bear Went over the Mountain
Bibbidi-Bobbidi-Boo
Bingo
Black Is the Color
Blow the Man Down
The Caisson Song

Charlie over the Ocean
Clementine
Deaf Woman's Courtship
Do Your Ears Hang Low?
Don't Fence Me In
Down in the Valley
Eensy Weensy Spider
Ezekial Saw De Wheel
Go Tell Aunt Rhody
Goodbye, Old Paint
Ha, Ha, This-a-Way
He's Got the Whole World in His
    Hands
Home on the Range
Hush, Little Baby
If I Had a Hammer
I'm a Little Teapot
It's Not Easy Being Green
I've Been Working on the Railroad
Jingle Bells
John Jacob Jingleheimer Schmidt
Johnnie, Get Your Hair Cut
Kum-Ba-Yah
Little David, Play on Your Harp
The Long-Legged Sailor
Lucy Locket
Mama Don't Allow
Marching to Pretoria
The Marine's Hymn
Mary Wore Her Red Dress
Michael, Row the Boat Ashore
The Mocking Bird Song
The More We Get Together
My Little Rooster
The Noble Duke of York
O, Susanna
Old Brass Wagon
Old Joe Clark
Old MacDonald
Old Texas

Over the River and through the Wood
Paw Paw Patch
The Riddle Song
Sally Go round the Sun
She'll Be Comin' round the Mountain
Shortnin' Bread
Skip to My Lou
Sourwood Mountain
The Star-Spangled Banner
This Land Is Your Land
This Old Man
A Tisket, a Tasket
Under the Sea
Wind up the Apple Tree
Witch, Witch
With a Little Help from My Friends
Yankee Doodle

SAMPLE LESSON, CHAPTER 2

LESSON OVERVIEW: This lesson integrates creative drama and music activities with economics content. Players will use a name game, noisy story, found and body sounds, and singing to learn about occupations.

RECOMMENDED GRADE: 2

CONTENT AREAS: drama/theatre, music, and economics

INSTRUCTIONAL OBJECTIVES:

- Players will be able to identify businesses and jobs in their local community. (Economics)
- Players will assume roles that exhibit concentration and contribute to the action of classroom dramatizations based upon personal experience and imagination. (Drama/theatre)
- Players will use a variety of sound sources, including traditional sounds, nontraditional sounds available in the classroom, and body sounds. (Music)

LENGTH OF LESSON: thirty minutes

ACTIVITIES AND PROCEDURES:

Preparation: Review these types of activities in the chapter.

Name Game: When I Grow Up

Players sit in a circle. The first person says his name and what he wants to be when he grows up. The person next to him repeats what the first player has said and then states her name and what she wants to be when she grows up. The game continues until everyone has had a turn.

Example:

Player #1: My name is Todd and I want to be an artist.

Player #2: His name is Todd and he wants to be an artist. My name is Courtney and I want to be a detective.

Noisy Story: "Sally's First Day of School"

This story can be played with children divided into groups of five. All players should make the sounds of the children in the story.

Sally:	Mother:
"What a day!"	"Now, dear"
Bus: "Honk honk"	School: "Time to learn"
Teacher: "Hello"	Children: "Yea!"

It was a new school* year and today was the first day. As Sally* waited for the bus,* she felt nervous. Sally's* mother* waited with her. "Don't worry," Mother* said reassuringly. Soon the bus* came around the corner and stopped. Sally* waved good-bye to her mother* and got on the bus.* There were many children* on the bus.* The children* were laughing and talking excitedly.

At school,* Sally* found her classroom. Her teacher* greeted Sally* and the other children.* "Welcome back to school,*" said the teacher.* "We're going to have a wonderful year together."

All morning, the teacher* helped Sally* and the other children.* The teacher* gave the children* crayons, and they made pictures. The teacher* sang a song, and Sally* and the other children* learned the song, too. The children* listened as the teacher* read a story. Sally* thought that the teacher* had a beautiful voice.

Sally* could hardly believe it when it was time to go home. She had enjoyed being with the teacher* and the other children.* As Sally* boarded the bus,* she couldn't wait to tell her mother* about her day. Sally* had enjoyed seeing the other children* after the long summer vacation. Sally* liked her teacher.* This year, school* was going to be fun!

Noisy Story Replay:
"Sally's First Day of School"
Replay the noisy story by substituting found sounds or body sounds for the starred words. The example below offers some suggestions for substitutions.

Sally: clap twice	Mother: deep sigh ("ah")
Bus: stomp feet quickly	School: click pen tops
Teacher: tap pencils on desks twice	Children: slap thighs rapidly

Body and Found Sound:
Accompaniment to Work Song
Sing "I've Been Working on the Railroad" as a group. Next, invite players to select found sounds to illustrate the following sounds of the song:

"working on the railroad"
"pass the time away"
"whistle blowing"
"rise so early in the morn"
"captain shouting"
"Dinah blow your horn"

Sing the song again with players substituting found sounds for specific phrases. For example, once the players find sounds for "working on the railroad," they being singing, as follows: "I've been," followed by the sounds; "all the live long day / I've been," followed by the same found sounds. Sounds for "pass the time away" are then inserted in lieu of singing that phrase, and the process continues.

ASSESSMENT: Complete the rubric shown in table 2.2.

NOTE
1. "Rhythm Lesson #5," Munchkins and Music, posted September 19, 2008, munchkinsandmusic.blogspot.com/2008/09/rhythm-lesson-5.html (accessed May 11, 2010).

Table 2.2. Rubric for Sample Lesson

	Yes	No	In part
Players identified those occupations in the lesson that are found in their local community.			
Players maintained concentration during the lesson.			
Players appropriately used found sounds or body sounds.			

CHAPTER 3

Listening and Seeing Imaginatively

THERE IS NO LIMIT TO OUR IDEAS, PLANS, and visions when we imagine. This ability is such a gift that it fully deserves to be nurtured and not taken for granted. The power of imagination increases human potential no matter what the chosen field; it is not solely the domain of artists. Imaginative growth is stimulated by sensory awareness (especially active listening and seeing), sensitivity, and concentration. This chapter contains activities that will assist the leader and players in using the treasures of the intellect and the imagination.

INTRODUCING BASIC CREATIVE DRAMA SKILLS

Creative drama involves skill building. Preliminary work includes forming rapport with the group, establishing a creative climate, and warming up the players. From here, the leader will introduce another layer of skills: **concentration**, **visualization**, and social interaction. When they are not easily distracted and have confidence, players are likely to be more fully engaged in activities. As they enter into more advanced work, such as creating characters and dramatizing stories, these activities will serve them well. Most leaders find that activities are played more successfully when a solid foundation of basic skills is in place.

In order to help players realize their abilities, the leader should use early sessions to facilitate skill development. These types of activities can be reintroduced and replayed in future sessions, even if these later sessions are more complex in nature. Each time skill-building activities occur, players should demonstrate increased self-assurance and greater depth of involvement. Players should display more imaginative responses and the ability to work collaboratively.

CONCENTRATION (LOWER/UPPER LEVELS)

It is not unusual, particularly in early sessions, for players to giggle or to become easily distracted. These behaviors often signal a lack of involvement, as do restlessness, embarrassed whispering, and superficial responses to activities. Such reactions are generally a result of short attention spans or discomfort caused by not knowing what is expected. Incorporating concentration activities into early sessions encourages involvement. Concentration exercises should be played regularly. By repeating activities, the leader assists players in focusing and maintaining concentration for longer periods of time.

Concentration Activity:
I'm Going Out West
With players seated in a circle, the leader begins by saying, "I'm going out west, and

33

I'm going to take . . . ," and then naming an object. The player to the left repeats the phrase and the leader's object, then adds an object. The next player repeats the phrase, the leader's object, and the first player's object, and adds an object. The game continues in this fashion, with players repeating the phrase and all objects in order, and then adding their own.

Example:

> Leader: I'm going out west and I'm going to take a horse.
>
> Player 1: I'm going out west and I'm going to take a horse and a bucket.
>
> Player 2: I'm going out west and I'm going to take a horse, a bucket, and a canteen.
>
> Player 3: I'm going out west and I'm going to take a horse, a bucket, a canteen, and a rope.

The leader may find that, as more objects are added in this example, they relate less to the western theme. Objects such as beach balls, kites, and cars may be added. This is acceptable, as emphasis should be on remembering objects, not on adhering to the theme.

When leading this activity, there are a few things to keep in mind. Eye contact, if culturally appropriate, is helpful in connecting player to object. For instance, in the example, Player 3 would look at Player 2 when remembering "canteen," at Player 1 when remembering "bucket," and at the leader when remembering "horse." Further, if a player forgets, other players will often whisper or pantomime objects. When supportively helping others to remember, players are engaging in teamwork. If someone really cannot continue, it becomes the next player's turn. The positive nature of assistance

and group effort should be stressed; there should be no sense of failure. As with all creative drama games, the objective is not to confuse or cause players to drop out until there is a "winner." The importance of competition is minimized in a creative climate.

There may be times when a player has difficulty remembering and others will giggle. This happens most frequently when the list of objects has become long. The leader should point out that, almost without exception, players are laughing *with* rather than *at* the player, because they are *empathizing* (feeling what another feels). The **empathetic response** is a shared, not a derogatory, reaction.

Finally, with young children or novice players, it may be helpful to divide into small groups of five or six people. Players generally can remember a short list and, as they become more proficient, increase the size of their list by going around the circle and adding objects more than once.

Concentration Activity:
Imaginary Ball Toss
Players stand in a circle. The leader begins by tossing an imaginary ball to one of the players, who then catches it. That player tosses it to another, and so on until the ball is "dropped" or the leader ends the game. Attention should be given to the ball's size, shape, weight, and composition, as well as to the tossing speed. Players try to relate to the object as if it were really there.

For some groups, beginning with an imaginary ball will be difficult. If this happens, practice by using the real object, tossing it to players at various points in the circle, and then removing it. Players can then repeat the activity in pantomime, maintaining the ball's size and shape and the tossing pattern.

Interest can be added to this activity by changing the ball's characteristics. It might, for example, become very heavy, lighter than air, fluffy, made of glass, very hot, or very cold. These changes allow players to use their imaginations and relate to the object in different ways. With each successive playing, the tossing sequences should grow longer.

The imaginary ball toss is designed to encourage teamwork and to deepen concentration. Players must be attentive so that they can follow the direction of the ball. They must also be aware of safety rules. Hard throws, great leaps in the air, and slams are inappropriate even in a pantomimed activity.

Concentration Activity: Mirroring

Mirroring is done in pairs playing in unison. One player is assigned the role of initiator, the other the role of mirror. The players face each other and, as the initiator produces a movement, the mirror imitates it. Players coordinate their movements as closely as possible so that it is difficult to tell who is leading the movement and who is following. The leader may wish to model the activity before playing begins in earnest.

Example:

The initiator performs the following sequence of actions: (1) raises right arm, then lowers it; (2) raises left arm; (3) moves right arm to the side, then returns it to waist; (4) raises and lowers left leg; and (5) lowers left arm. The mirror does these movements simultaneously, so that action appears to be closely coordinated.

When mirroring, emphasis should be on eye contact. If players are embarrassed by looking directly into each other's eyes, laughter may result. Those laughing should stop, regain their composure, and begin again when they are ready.

In addition to developing concentration skills, mirroring also builds trust and teamwork. As players become more adept, they will want to switch roles so that each has a chance to both lead and follow. This can be done by stopping the activity and switching or, for more skilled players, passing the lead back and forth without interruption. Using this method, there must be no verbal cuing of intentions; the lead alternates only through movement. As mastery builds, players can add facial expressions and increase mobility. Ultimately, they may be able to coordinate sounds, words, and movement around the **playing space** where the activity occurs. They will find that the more they are attuned to their partners, the more they are able to anticipate actions. Mirroring can become quite complex.

Concentration Activity: Mirroring, Variation

All of the players assume the role of the mirror while the session leader initiates the actions. This simplified technique benefits young players who find working in pairs difficult. Gross motor movements (e.g., full body, twisting, stooping) work especially well.

Concentration Activity: Shadowing

An individual player pantomimes an action or series of actions while the others watch. A player, for example, could pantomime walking into a room, closing a door, picking up a book, sitting in a chair, and reading. Then a second player is selected from among the observers. That player tries to recreate the first player's actions. Shadowing requires attention to detail and is recommended for more experienced players.

Concentration Activity:
Puppet and Puppeteer
This activity is played much like mirroring and is a good way to illustrate responsibility and teamwork. Players again work in pairs. One assumes the role of the puppet, the other the puppeteer. Together, they decide where imaginary strings are placed on the marionette. Popular locations are the top of the head, the end of each hand, each elbow, each foot, the knees, and the shoulders. When the puppeteer moves a string, the puppet responds by moving the body part as directed.

All movement is pantomimed, and the puppeteer never actually touches the puppet. Two or more strings can be manipulated together, such as raising a hand and a foot. The puppeteer must be careful not to let the puppet fall or to resort to uncomfortable contortions. Players do not speak, but should attempt to communicate through strong and direct eye contact. Once partners really become attuned to each other, they enjoy making the marionette walk and dance. Replaying accommodates switching roles.

CLASSROOM MANAGEMENT

Creative drama and music activities have the potential to produce a great deal of excitement and action. While these often encourage a lively response, this should not be confused with chaos. Safety, respect for others, focus, and cooperation are necessary.

When the players become too noisy or too wild, or when it is necessary to stop an activity, **control** should be pleasantly but firmly reestablished. Its incorporation into play should be positive, not punitive. If possible, it should be built into the structure of the lesson. Some leaders favor a *control word*, such as "**freeze**."

USING A CONTROL WORD:

Leader:
- When you hear me say "freeze," stop where you are. That way, I'll know that everyone has finished and we can talk about your interpretations.

Other leaders like to establish control by flicking the lights in the room or by blowing a whistle. Some simply hold up their hands. More inventive control devices include a dial on cardboard that moves from a "freeze" to an "unfreeze" position. This is called a *freeze-o-meter*. Stop signs or similar visual reminders also might be used. Regardless of the method, control is designed to keep things running smoothly.

QUIETING ACTIVITIES

The purpose of **quieting activities** is to calm. They are sometimes used to conclude lessons or individual exercises. They can be interspersed between activities that produce a highly energetic response. They are an important tool in pacing a session. Often, pantomime activities are used for this purpose. The leader might, for instance, tell the players to "imagine that you are a snowman and melt in the hot sun." They would all slowly sink to the floor and lie quietly until given further instructions. Another example might be, "You are a campfire slowly burning out until you are completely extinguished." Again, players' energy ebbs until they are quiet and still.

HEIGHTENING THE IMAGINATION: ABSTRACT/CONCRETE IMAGES (LOWER/UPPER LEVELS)

Through creative drama, players can use their own bodies or can mold others into shapes and designs. In this way, they communicate ideas that it might otherwise be difficult to express. Players can create either **abstract** or **concrete** images. By positioning others physically, players can create entire compositions and also see how each individual part contributes to the design as a whole. The players will realize that each person has something important to add and that, by working together, all have had a part in the creative process.

Most young people have an interest in such art projects as drawing, using clay, and constructing models. When given people to work with instead of traditional media, players can become artists. The leader can call attention to

- space (various levels, composition, viewer perspective, distance, and relative importance of foreground, middle, and background);
- shapes (geometric forms such as triangles, rectangles, and circles, varying in size, color, value, and complexity);
- directional lines (planes moving vertically, horizontally, circularly, or in some variation or combination of these);
- value (variations in lightness and darkness);
- how elements complement or contrast with each other;
- the emotional content of the work.

Concrete activities focus on real and identifiable objects. Abstract activities allow players to envision less representational ideas. In a concrete body sculpture, for example, players might form an automobile (becoming the seats, wheels, and steering wheel). In an abstract body sculpture, they might interpret "yellow" as bright and happy, and their sculpture would reflect a lot of open body positions.

Abstract Activity: Body Sculptures

In this exercise, the leader supplies the stimulus or the players decide on an abstract concept such as an emotion. They come, one at a time, to the center of the room. They use their bodies to freeze in a position that reflects the concept. Their stances should fit with positions that others have already taken. When several players have created a strong overall image, the rest of the group can discuss how the completed picture reflects the original concept.

Example 1:

Leader: "Come to the center of the room, one at a time, and show with your body how you look when you are *happy*."

Player 1: Comes to the center, stands at attention and smiles.

Player 2: Comes to the center, stands to the right of Player 1 with feet spread apart and both arms raised upward.

Player 3: Comes to the center, stands to the left of Player 1, places one hand on Player 1's shoulder, and raises the other arm upward.

Player 4: Comes to the center, sits in front of Player 1, and raises both hands in "*V* for victory" signs.

Discussion: The group should notice the upward direction and the openness of the bodies, which they might relate to feeling happy.

Example 2:

Leader: "Come to the center of the room, one at a time, and show how the color *red* makes you feel."

Player 1: Comes to the center of the room, stands with feet close together, arms at sides, with fists clenched.

Player 2: Comes to the center, stands behind Player 1, places arms around Player 1's waist.

Player 3: Comes to the center, stands in front of and faces Player 1. Player 3 raises clenched hands in front of Player 1's face.

The group should notice the tight arrangement of bodies and the closed positions of limbs. Players might equate anger with the feeling suggested by the color red.

The above are simply suggestions. Each player's position should express individual feelings and contribute to the sculpture as a whole. The leader should emphasize the word "*show*" in the instructions. As in all creative drama activities, "showing" is the basis for action.

Note that this sort of activity demands attention to safety. Classroom management should be established before beginning play. Guidelines can be introduced without stifling creative response.

Concrete Activity: Living Pictures
The directions for this activity are the same as for "Body Sculptures," except that players work with concrete ideas. Some interesting subjects are planes, castles, forests, and playgrounds. To integrate language arts, players might create pictures of the settings of favorite stories. The best source for living picture ideas is often the players themselves.

Concrete Activities: Machines
One player comes to the center of the room and begins a motion. Another player joins, adding a new motion. Others join, one at a time, each adding a new movement. When a sufficient number have become a part of the machine, the leader "freezes" the device. Players can then name and describe the object.

To make this activity more challenging, the players could be told to add a motion and a sound. Each must be original. No one is allowed to imitate another player. This will produce some unusual sights and noises! In another variation, upon entering the machine each person must touch some other player. This allows all players to be connected physically. One might take a position that requires placing a hand on another player's back or a foot alongside a classmate's foot. Conversely, a "no touching" rule would mean that there is no physical contact within the machine.

Similar to "Body Sculptures" and "Living Pictures," "Machines" is an activity that encourages players to use their imaginations. Their creation can be a recognizable machine or pure fantasy. Although this is an animated activity, movement needs to be confined to personal space within the machine. Those players who are not actually a part of the machine may be asked to name it or to describe its function. It is acceptable to have several names or functions for each machine, as not everyone will see the same thing in the design.

Abstract/Concrete Activity: Tug-of-War
This version of a tug-of-war is commonly played with two teams and an imaginary rope. After teams are formed, players spend a few minutes planning positions and strategy. The leader should check that all have a clear and shared vision of the size and the shape of the rope. If this presents difficulty, a real rope can be used once or twice and then removed. (Players then can recall the rope's properties.)

To start, the imaginary rope is on the floor and teams line up facing each other. On the leader's count of three, the players pick up the imaginary rope and begin. Each team tries to get the rope away from the other. The effort continues until one team is successful, players on one or both teams fall, the rope breaks, or the leader declares a draw.

To encourage the players to really see the rope in their imaginations, the leader may wish to **sidecoach** (a technique for deepening involvement) with comments and questions such as "Both teams are pulling hard!" or "How does the rope feel as it moves through your hand?" Side-coaching questions can prompt thought about sensory awareness. All players need to see the same rope if the activity is to be successful.

This version of a tug-of-war stimulates imagination, promotes teamwork, fosters concentration, builds recognition of muscle response, and encourages sensory awareness. Players must be alert to their teammates' actions as well as the responses of the other team. They should realize that if a rope is pulled taut and one team doesn't budge when the other pulls, the rope will snap in half and break or be jerked away, usually causing people to fall.

Because of the physical demands of the activity, the leader must attend to safety. Managing behavior can be creatively incorporated into the activity in a number of ways. One approach is to play in slow motion. Another is to develop a broadcasting scenario, in which the leader or a responsible player provides commentary as if the contest were being broadcast. Such commentary can moderate pace and often suggests specific movements for the teams.

When working with large groups, dividing the class into several teams and playing in a round robin fashion (two competing at a time) makes classroom management easier. Under normal circumstances, teams with more than five or six players tend to be unwieldy. Regardless of the number of teams, the leader should stress the importance of **ensemble play** (working together for the good of the team rather than for personal recognition). Cooperating rather than competing is paramount.

Initially, there should be no sound for this activity. During replays, however, players may adapt the contest and often enjoy adding cheering and words of encouragement that build teamwork. Replay is also a time for players to develop and try new strategies that stress the importance of working together.

MUSICAL ECHOES
(LOWER/UPPER LEVELS)

A number of very enjoyable activities involve echoing rhythms and the imagination of new rhythms in "conversational" contexts. The conversations may start with simple echoes and progress to sophisticated musical **phrases** traded back and forth between players. While playing the "Simon Says" game, players sharpen their listening skills and refine skills in sequencing and chaining rhythms. The following games range from simple to complex and are offered as foundational to help players develop sophisticated listening and performance skills.

With the exception of "No Peek Challenge," the players generally watch and listen to the leader when performing echo games. Players should wait until it is their turn to repeat. To ensure success, the leader should provide a clear entrance cue. Preparing the rhythm by counting "1, 2, rea-dy, go!" helps establish the tempo. Or a pointing gesture toward the group, for example, will give them a definite cue to begin and will prevent players from starting their responses too soon.

Echo Activity: Simon Says

The leader claps a pattern such as the rhythm to "Rain, Rain, Go Away." The players, relying on their ears alone, echo the leader. (The leader does not repeat the clapping pattern when the players repeat.) Figure 3.1 shows some simple patterns for the echo game.

Echo Activity: Name That Tune

The leader begins this activity by clapping patterns of longer duration, such as half of the rhythm to the tune "Happy Birthday." The players echo the leader. After disclosing that the rhythm belongs to a song they know, the leader claps the rhythm for the entire song and asks the players to identify the tune that goes along with that rhythm.

Some songs, such as "Jingle Bells," "The Star Spangled Banner," and "Are You Sleeping?," are easy for players to identify. Players will soon be able to lead this activity on their own.

Echo Activity: Chain Game

In this echo game, the leader performs a pattern, and while the players echo the pattern, the leader begins to perform another. This will create a **round**-type echo. A simple example appears in figure 3.2.

While it might be easiest to limit the sounds to clapping at first, it is interesting and challenging to combine two or three body sounds (incorporating things like snapping or patchen) in this activity. Change the sound sources every two beats. For example, the leader may clap

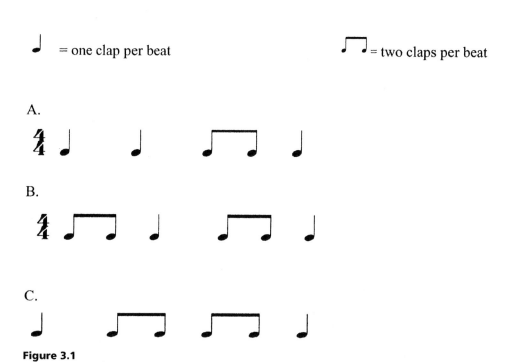

Figure 3.1

Key: ♩ = one clap per beat

♫ = two claps per beat

𝄽 = one rest per beat

Figure 3.2

the first two notes and patchen the next set. Rhythms from familiar rounds, such as "Are You Sleeping?," "Old Texas," or "Hey, Ho, Nobody Home," are successful starters. With multiple sounds, this game is for advanced players.

Echo Activity: No Peek Challenge
The leader uses multiple body sounds while the players, facing in another direction, listen. Since they will not see the leader, they will have to listen analytically and rely on their ears to distinguish a clap from a stomp. Beginning with short patterns, the leader limits the exercise to just two distinct sounds to assure success. Gradually, different sounds within more complex rhythms can be added for greater challenge. Before long, players are ready to serve as leaders.

Figure 3.3 provides an example of a "No Peek Challenge." Note the simplicity of rhythm (single beat) and limited number of body sounds.

RHYTHMIC DIALOGUES (LOWER/UPPER LEVELS)

Musical conversations become more interesting if they go beyond echoes and **repetition**. The following games involve some echoing and introduce basic **improvisation** (inventing new patterns). A greater exploration of improvisation occurs in chapter 6. It's important to master simple dialogues, however, before moving on to complex ones.

All of the activities using body sounds can be transferred to found sound sources (see chapter 2). In fact, once players have explored body sounds, found sounds are natural extensions.

The major role of the leader is to guide exploration and refine listening skills. To assist in classroom management, players need to understand the purpose and procedures of each activity. Therefore, it is very important to clearly state directions and demonstrate model behaviors. It is sometimes helpful to ask players to

Key: ♩ = 1 beat

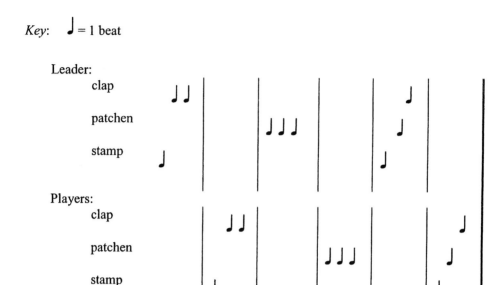

Figure 3.3

restate the directions in their own words. This allows for additional clarity and verifies comprehension.

Leaders need to plan strategic questions to nurture this exploration. During these activities, open-ended questions are best, such as "What would happen if this pattern were performed in outer space?"; "Where could we find a sound heard under water?"; "What new patterns can be invented to show a different mood?"; or "If that object could talk, how would it sound if it were happy? Lonely? Excited? Afraid?"

Finally, how the leader participates often determines the players' attitudes and behaviors. If the leader is curious, inquisitive, thoughtful, open, and positive in recognizing players' contributions, the players will also reflect appropriate attitudes and pursue their discoveries like true artists.

Rhythmic Dialogue Activity: Persistence
The leader starts by clapping the rhythmic pattern to phrases of "Mary Had a Little Lamb." The players echo it. The players must clap this pattern as their response to all rhythmic ideas the leader performs. Remind them that they are "stuck" on this rhythm. (They are not to echo the leader.) Regardless of what rhythm they hear the leader clap, they must answer with the original pattern.

After practicing the group answer several times (see figure 3.4), this dialogue might be performed with body sounds or found sounds.

Rhythmic Dialogue Activity:
Rhythmic Rondo
A **rondo** is a musical form that has a section that recurs after each contrasting section. The first section (A) presents the theme, and it follows every new section. The group performs a rhythmic rondo beginning with the group theme (A), then individuals **solo** with different rhythms. After each solo part, the group restates their section (A), which repeats.

Again, this activity may be limited to one body sound, or it may be expanded

Key: ♩ = 1 beat

Practice group answer: ♫ ♫ ♫ ♩

Leader: ♩ ♩ ♫ ♩

Group: ♫ ♫ ♫ ♩

Leader: ♫ ♩ ♩ ♩

Group: ♫ ♫ ♫ ♩

Leader: ♩ ♫ ♫ ♩

Group: ♫ ♫ ♫ ♩

Figure 3.4

to two or three. It is recommended that the patterns, as in the examples shown in figure 3.5, be kept relatively brief. Practicing the group pattern several times will also help players retain it.

Rhythmic Dialogue Activity: Q & A
The leader states a rhythmic phrase by clapping a pattern for a specific player to answer. The player improvises an "answer." The examples in figure 3.6 illustrate the question and answer dialogue.

Rhythmic Dialogue Activity: Whale's Tails
This dialogue activity is similar to "I'm Going Out West." It is a line game that begins with one player creating a rhythm pattern. The second player repeats the first rhythm pattern, then adds a new one. The third player must replicate the first two patterns before adding another. The game continues until an error is made. Following an error, the game starts over with the next player.

SOUND JOURNALS (LOWER/UPPER LEVELS)

Sounds are as varied as colors. Sounds deserve careful listening *and* thinking in the creative process. Some sounds go together in a pleasing fashion. Other sounds clash like competing colors. Some sounds are loud and bright. They can overpower other sounds. Others are gentle and subtle. They can hide under other sounds. These characteristics are known as **timbre**.

Listening activities make players aware of the different timbres by focusing on those that are in the foreground (more obvious) and those that are in the background (less obvious). First, however, the leader must help players pay attention to the clock ticking, the hum of fluorescent lights, the birds singing, or traffic noises—sounds that tend to be relegated to background noise. Then, with more attentive listening skills, players can appreciate sounds on a more sophisticated level. Such a progression will develop all

A simple rondo is organized into the following scheme:

Group—Player 1—Group—Player 2—Group, etc.
  (A)   (B)   (A)   (C)   (A)

The "A" theme, or group pattern, recurs after each new section. An example of a rhythmic rondo might be:

Figure 3.5

Key: ♩ = one beat

♩ = two beats

♩. = three beats

Leader:

Player's possible response:

Figure 3.6

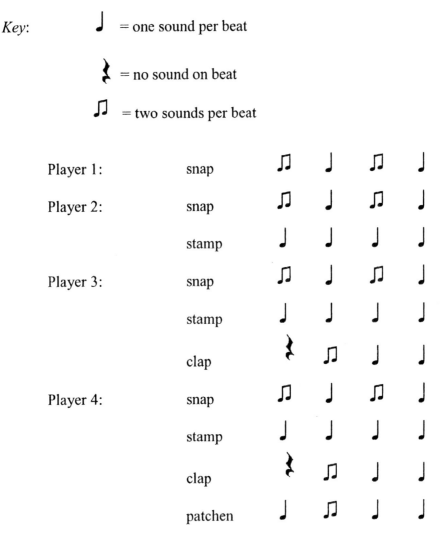

Key:

♩ = one sound per beat

𝄽 = no sound on beat

♫ = two sounds per beat

Player 1:	snap	♫	♩	♫	♩
Player 2:	snap	♫	♩	♫	♩
	stamp	♩	♩	♩	♩
Player 3:	snap	♫	♩	♫	♩
	stamp	♩	♩	♩	♩
	clap	𝄽	♫	♩	♩
Player 4:	snap	♫	♩	♫	♩
	stamp	♩	♩	♩	♩
	clap	𝄽	♫	♩	♩
	patchen	♩	♫	♩	♩

Figure 3.7

players' listening skills, on a continuum from marginal to analytical skill levels (see chapter 2).

Our everyday environment has many different sounds, and they characteristically represent special locations, for example, the toy store, Laundromat, supermarket, and car wash. Once sounds become more apparent, their critical differences can be analyzed. The sound's pitch level (high or low), dynamics (loud or soft), intensity (dull or piercing), and duration (long or short) are just a few of the characteristics that distinguish a baby's sigh from a monster's screech. During a nature walk, on the school bus, or while listening (only) to the television, all sorts of sounds can be rediscovered merely by drawing deliberate attention to them. Listening with one's eyes closed and concentrating specifically on sound cues are ways to focus attention.

Maintaining a sound journal is an intriguing and effective way to document what is heard, understood, and felt. A sound journal shows the leader what the players process aurally. In a journal, players collect and record the sounds they hear at various times and then describe them. It might be useful to ask players to make a record of their sounds each day for a week in a notebook. Later, they can classify a sound by telling something about it and drawing what it looks like.

Drawing helps players visualize sounds so that they can recall them later for composition purposes. (Composition activities are explored fully in chapter 7.) Another value in the task of graphically representing sounds is that the players can begin to make judgments about the combinations of sounds. They will see that one sound will conflict with or cover up other sounds.

Example:
Monday

What kind of sound did you hear?	A jet flew by.
Tell something about it:	It roared like a lion and then purred like a kitty cat.
Draw what it sounds like:	

Figure 3.8

What kind of sound did you hear?	Windshield wipers on the bus.
Tell something about it:	They go back and forth, over and over again, a-tick, a-tack, a-tick, a-tack. They screech when there isn't enough rain on the windows. They take a nap when the bus driver turns them off.
Draw what it sounds like:	On

Figure 3.9

Screeching

Figure 3.10

Off

What kind of sound did you hear?	The fire alarm at school rings.
Tell something about it:	It goes *ennnnnnnnnnnnnn.*
Draw what it sounds like:	_____

SAMPLE LESSON, CHAPTER 3
LESSON OVERVIEW: This lesson integrates creative drama and music activities with physical education content. Players will use physical skills, imagination, concentration, and teamwork in this lesson with a sports theme.
RECOMMENDED GRADE: 4
CONTENT AREAS: drama/theatre, music, and physical education
INSTRUCTIONAL OBJECTIVES:

- Students will demonstrate competency in motor skills and movement patterns that are needed to perform a variety of physical activities. (Physical education)

- Students will use variations of locomotor and nonlocomotor movement. (Drama/theatre)
- Students will echo short rhythms and melodic patterns and will rhythmically improvise "answers." (Music)

LENGTH OF LESSON: thirty to forty-five minutes

ACTIVITIES AND PROCEDURES:

Preparation: Review these types of activities in the chapter.

Concentration Activity:
Imaginary Ball Toss

Players stand in a circle and begin the game by tossing a ball. The leader then takes the ball and asks them to replicate the pattern using an imaginary ball. Once players can do this successfully, new properties are assigned to the imaginary ball, and the players toss it. Encourage them to vary the pattern rather than just tossing the ball to the next person.

Below are suggestions for changing the size, shape, or weight of the ball.

The ball is . . .

the shape of a football
the size and weight of a beach ball
made of popcorn
the weight of a Ping Pong ball
sticky
made of melting snow
rubbery

Rhythmic Dialogue Activity:
Ball Players' Game

Using a variety of balls, players may bounce them to the beat of a drum, to chants or poems, or to recorded music. Approach practice with larger balls (e.g., volleyball size) at a moderate tempo. Once players

develop their skills, vary the activity by using smaller balls and faster tempos.

Concentration Activity: Mirroring

Paired players select a sport together and then decide who will be the mirror and who the initiator. They pantomime dressing for the sport, with the mirror reflecting the initiator's actions.

Try the activity with these sports: baseball, football, track, swimming, tennis, hockey, and ice skating.

Rhythmic Dialogue Activity:
Ball Conversation

Players take turns "bouncing" rhythmic messages to one another in a conversational style. One player improvises a pattern, which is echoed by a second player. Both players are then encouraged to improvise original patterns.

Fourth graders should be able to pass one ball between two children; but if they find this difficult, the leader can furnish each player with a ball so that conversations can "flow."

Concrete Activity: Machines

Using their bodies, players create a machine that can be used in a new sport of their own invention. Sound is optional. After forming the machine, they should demonstrate and explain how it works.

Concrete Activity: Tug-of-War

Several volunteers can serve as broadcasters who provide the "play-by-play" for a tug-of-war being televised. Other players form the competing teams.

Sound Journal

Players should listen to the following sounds and then describe and draw them in a sound journal.

a bat hitting a baseball
a foot hitting a football
an iron striking a golf ball
a basketball hitting the hoop
  board

a tennis ball hitting the racquet
a beach ball hitting the sand

ASSESSMENT: Complete the rubric shown in table 3.1.

Table 3.1. Rubric for Sample Lesson

	Yes	No	In part
Players have used a variety of motor skills and movements during these activities.			
Players have used imagination and maintained concentration during these activities.			
Players have successfully echoed, improvised, and demonstrated discriminating listening skills.			
Players have worked well with others.			

CHAPTER 4

Expressing Creatively without Words

In this chapter, creative drama and music activities focus on physical rather than verbal expression. When players can use their bodies comfortably, they expand their expressive repertoire and build a solid foundation for later work. In the following activities, both leaders and players tune up, tone up, and communicate without sound.

Nonverbal communication is an important way of sending messages. Our postures, gestures, facial expressions, and other physical movements reveal thoughts, feelings, and actions. People are almost constantly in motion. Some movements involve gross motor skills, such as walking, running, and jogging. Some involve fine motor skills, such as tapping fingers and toes. Humans also embellish speech with intentional gestures and facial expressions. They are capable of sending clear and strong messages through the use of their bodies.

When verbal and nonverbal messages are in conflict, it is the nonverbal that is perceived as more credible. Communication tools are voice and body, but developing the latter ensures that players will not be overly reliant on the former. Players will learn to send and receive complete messages by adequately developing both verbal and nonverbal tools of expression.

CREATIVE MOVEMENT (UPPER/LOWER LEVELS)

Music innately brings out movement in children. They spontaneously and freely respond to the mood, tempo (speed), melodic direction (up and down), and dynamics (volume). Sometimes the movements appear unencumbered and random; at other times, there seems to be a deliberate connection between the movements and the music. Further, for many tactile learners, music becomes more expressive when connected to creative movement.

Before players can derive the most enjoyment from moving creatively, they must (1) listen analytically, and (2) concentrate on their movements. Leaders may facilitate two types of activities for players: *structured* and *unstructured.* Each of these serves different ends. Structured experiences build a vocabulary of fundamental movements. They occur within defined parameters such as starting and stopping together, pacing transitions from one movement to another, and keeping pace with a partner or others. Unstructured activities require more independent and original thinking.

Previous activities have concentrated on attentive listening skills. The following activities build upon players' abilities to discriminate among sounds, leading to informed and sensitive movement experiences. Unlike other forms of musical communication, they will not need instruments or lyrics for singing. They will need, however, to explore space and time with their bodies and especially their ears.

Creative movement to music is not as simple as providing music and asking players to move. There are just a few guidelines. Select a brief composition (not more than five minutes) or only a short segment of a longer piece. The first time players listen, invite them to listen for the mood or "**soundscape**." "How does the music make you feel?" "What do you think is happening within the music?" Encourage them to imagine while listening, keeping their eyes closed.

MOVING TO MUSIC

In guiding creative movement to music, emphasize the following rules:

- Observe the parameters for movement (what space is open).
- Respect the space of others.
- Be careful around furniture/ equipment.
- Avoid risky movements.
- Match movement to music, poem, or story.

Ask players to listen a second time and to plan their movements. Now it is time to *think* about what they hear. "What do you want to 'say' about this music in your movements?" the leader might ask. The leader can help direct some creative movement choices by asking open-ended questions about musical characteristics, such as, "How can we express that the music is moving up high?"; "If we tiptoe, what

might that communicate about the dynamics of the music?"; or "How can we move to show that the music has changed?"

Select music that has high potential for expressive response. Music that is stylistically too subtle or too monotonous is difficult for players to express. It is important to find the appropriate type of music to match the interest level and abilities of the group. Don't underestimate players' ability to respond creatively to a wide variety of music. Preview all music to determine whether it will fulfill the creative goals. Once successful creative movement has been experienced, the type of music needs to be varied to allow players to explore new moods and musical concepts. A list of recommended repertory is at the end of this chapter.

Leading Movement to Music
Creative responses are based upon a vocabulary of movements. Players should practice the "basics" and explore them anew. Ask players to think about learning to walk, for example, and to demonstrate as if they were learning the skill for the first time. This rediscovery process is fun and opens a new awareness to how expressive even the simplest of movements can be.

GUIDED LISTENING FOR CREATIVE MOVEMENT

- Have players listen to the music twice.
- First, listen for total impression with eyes closed.
- Listen again to the musical characteristics* and plan movements.

*Such as rhythm, beat, pitch level, tempo, melodic direction, and dynamics.

Movement Activity:
Getting to Know You

This exercise invites players to look at what is behind basic movements. Walking, for example, is pedantic for most people, both literally and figuratively. Or is it? Ask players to take a few walking steps and notice what body parts are involved. Focus their concentration upon feeling the movements while they keep their eyes closed. After taking a few "normal" walking steps, does it feel normal? If players notice a difference, this is precisely the desired outcome.

Next, invite players to think about how many different ways—and in how many directions—they can walk (e.g., in place, backwards, high-stepping, crisscrossing, in slow motion). After two to three minutes of group exploration, each player demonstrates a different walk. The leader starts by providing eight soft beats on the drum and allowing volunteers to model their original walks for the group.

Young players will want to imitate one another, so it may be desirable to have everyone mimic each new movement. Later, the leader may skillfully encourage originality and individuality. Once creative walks are exhausted, select another **fundamental movement** from the list below:

walk	hop
run	reach
march	pull
tiptoe	point
jump	gallop
twist	bend
push	skip
pull	lunge
jog	turn (quarter,
slide	half, etc.)
leap	whirl
kick	

Select two fundamental, contrasting movements per session. This will stretch the players' repertory.

Movement Activity: Hang Loose

In "Hang Loose," all players pretend they are marionettes whose strings are very loose. The leader announces the specific movement (such as jumping) and counts eight beats to provide think time. Encourage the group to consider a number of ways different people or things may jump. A frog, for example, jumps quite differently from a cheerleader, a grasshopper, a jack-in-the-box, or a basketball player. After the preparatory beats, players jump in their own ways for four beats. The leader may then invite players to share their movements for group practice and discussion.

Movement Activity: Domino Effect

Players select a fundamental movement, such as waving, and execute it one right after another in a line, to create the "Domino Effect." With some practice, they will coordinate their movements at just the right moment. It is also helpful to practice the movement in slow motion to create the right effect. Demonstrate the "Domino Effect" with five or six players while the rest of the group watches. Observers can critique the importance of coordinated effort.

Movement Activity: Tempo Tantrum

This game requires careful control of the movement's speed. The leader selects one movement (e.g., kicking), and the group practices it at a normal speed. After a faster preparatory count, they kick five times in fast-forward motion. Then contrast fast movements with slow-motion kicking. For a challenge, players can alternate tempos. Stressing that these movements are a form of communication, ask players to share their interpretations.

Movement Activity: Pattern Formation

When players have command of the fundamentals, they can begin combining them into simple expressive patterns. The leader starts with a basic pattern using two or three movements. The leader states how many times the pattern will be repeated and establishes the tempo with a four-beat preparation on a drum.

Example:

step, step, step, hop
(repeat pattern 4 times)

Even though all players are given the same directions, they may have a variety of interpretations. The leader should take advantage of the moment by pointing out creative differences.

When the players are ready, movements may combine upper- and lower-body motions. Players will soon be ready to improvise a series of eight movements in a pattern, to stretch their ability to concentrate, sequence, and recall. Below are some examples that can extend the repertory through more complex structures:

Examples:

push, reach, push, reach
(repeat 4 times)
hop on left, kick right, hop on right, kick left
(repeat 4 times)

PANTOMIME (LOWER/UPPER LEVELS)

Pantomime is the physical expression of thoughts, feelings, and actions. Players use their bodies, but not sound, to communicate. Players will find pantomime helpful for learning to comfortably use physical skills as activities become more complex. These exercises build confidence. Players will know that their physical choices communicate before they create **dialogue**.

Close **observation** of surroundings and human behaviors is fundamental for developing pantomime skills. The leader should emphasize the importance of seeing clearly and noting details. **Sensory awareness** (seeing, hearing, tasting, feeling, and smelling) and **imagination** (visualizing in the mind's eye) join concentration as factors necessary to success. The image should be clear in the player's mind to ensure recognition and not produce a guessing game.

Actions and emotions drive pantomime, and they should be expressed using active rather than passive verbs. Beginning with "Show me how you look when . . ." or "You are . . ." generates more action than "Be a . . ." Having something to do or show keeps players focused on making active choices, as illustrated in the following activities.

Pantomime Activity: Alphabet Game
Players will need adequate personal space for this unison activity. In unison play, everyone does the activity at the same time. In the "Alphabet Game," the leader selects a letter and calls out words that begin with it. Players pantomime the first thing that comes to mind. The leader then selects a new caller. After giving several words, that player selects another caller. The game continues in this fashion. Not repeating letters and limiting the number of words give more players a chance to call.

Example:

Leader: My letter is *a*: apple, acrobat, airplane.

Player 1: My letter is *r*: rabbit, roller skates, rope, rodeo.

Variations in the game can extend language arts skills. For example, use words with double meanings, such as *saw*.

Another variation targets vocabulary and spelling using words such as *eyeball, ivy,* and *aisle.* A third variation asks players to pantomime the opposite meaning of the word. If a mistake is made and others call attention to it, the leader can acknowledge the error but should quickly resume play.

Pantomime Activity: When You Know the Place, Join In

Many locations are recognizable because of what occurs there. To begin this exercise, one player comes to the center of the room and pantomimes an activity related to a specific place. As other players recognize the locale, they join as new characters engaged in different actions.

Example:

> Player 1: Pantomimes a baseball player who is up to bat.
>
> Player 2: Joins as the pitcher.
>
> Player 3: Joins as the catcher.
>
> Player 4: Joins as an umpire.

Other players may join as first, second, and third basemen, outfielders, shortstops, coaches, vendors, and fans. The location is a baseball park. Other locations that work well are the grocery store, the beach, the mall, and a school.

Pantomime Activity: Literal Phrases

Players can have fun while learning about language when they do this exercise. Start with a list of phrases that, when used literally, have different meanings. For example, the expression "come to a fork in the road" is used to mean selecting which direction to go. When literally interpreted, players would pantomime walking and picking up a fork from the road. Players may be momentarily stumped as

they clear away familiar usage. Once they grasp literal meaning, they pantomime the phrase. In addition to resulting in some humorous dramatic actions, this exercise challenges players to think about how language is used, how meanings change, semantics, and communication.

Examples:
> raining cats and dogs
> paint the town red
> lend an ear
> catch a train
> take a bath
> cross that bridge when you get to it
> hit the road

Pantomime Activity: Pantomime Sentences

Action is imperative in pantomime sentences. There must be something for the players to show or do. Simple sentences work best. Remember that players will need enough room to express themselves physically.

Examples:
> You are running in a marathon wearing shoes that are too tight for your feet.
> Show me how you would make the world's largest cake.
> You are a balloon blowing up and then deflating.
> You are a clown trying to make someone laugh.

Pantomime Activity: Sequence Game

Pantomime can be used to reinforce sequencing skills. Before playing sequence games, the leader will need to create a series of cards, each having a cue and an activity to pantomime. (The first card is an exception as it lists only an activity. Please see the example.) Cards should be distributed randomly to the players, who must watch carefully and identify their cues. Upon recognizing his or her cue as the action performed by another player, the next player comes to the center of the room.

A few simple guidelines will facilitate play. When pantomiming what is on their cards, players should face the rest of the group so that everyone can see clearly. Cards should not be numbered, as players would count rather than watch for clear and detailed actions. It is a good idea, however, to have a master cue sheet for the leader that notes the order of the cards. That way, if the sequence is disrupted, a quick check can reveal what happened. Writing the cue in one font or color at the top and the action in another font or color at the bottom is recommended. Wording of the action on one card and the cue on the following card should be the same.

If a player incorrectly identifies a cue and goes out of turn, the value of the activity is not lost. Leaders can use a sequencing game to discuss the difference between story events and **plot**. Plot is defined as dramatic events and the order in which they occur. In the story of "Cinderella," for example, the following are all story events. Their order, however, can alter the story and its **believability**.

Example 1:
1. Cinderella rides in a fine coach to the ball.
2. Cinderella dances with the prince.
3. Cinderella hears the clock strike, runs away, and loses her slipper.

Example 2:
1. Cinderella hears the clock strike, runs away, and loses her slipper.
2. Cinderella dances with the prince.
3. Cinderella rides in a fine coach to the ball.

Sequence games can be adapted to many content areas. Like the one that follows on communication, they can be written for specific topics. If players know or are reading a story, it can be divided into episodes, such as in the "Cinderella" example. Finally, as a recreational activity, sequence games will still do the job!

SEQUENCE GAMES AND READING

- Players have to read their cards silently to know the cues and actions.
- They must "read" nonverbal behaviors to identify cues.
- At the end of the game, all cards are read aloud.

Creative Movement with Poetry
Leaders can inspire players to move creatively to express poetry. The leader's role in facilitating movement experiences is to help the player communicate the mood or meaning of the poetry. Though literal movements may be explored first, advanced players should be encouraged to express feelings and ideas in abstract ways as well. After reading the poems below, the leader can ask for particular words or ideas that can be conveyed in movements. The poems may be recited while movements are added, or the movements may be performed after each line.

"Mighty Wind"
When you hear the wind a-blowing
Then it is surely time for knowing
That you should dress up warm and tight
And face the wind with all your might.

Table 4.1. Sequence game cards: "Communication"

You start the game. Come to the center of the room and pantomime a baby trying to let her mother know she's hungry.

The person before you has pantomimed a baby trying to let her mother know she's hungry.

You come to the center of the room and pantomime a cave man drawing a picture on a cave wall.

The person before you has pantomimed a cave man drawing a picture on a cave wall.

You come to the center of the room and pantomime serving as the town crier, walking down a street ringing a bell and shouting the news.

The person before you has pantomimed serving as the town crier, walking down a street ringing a bell and shouting the news.

You come to the center of the room and pantomime operating a printing press.

The person before you has pantomimed operating a printing press.

You come to the center of the room and pantomime acting in a silent movie.

The person before you has pantomimed acting in a silent movie.

You come to the center of the room and pantomime typing an e-mail message on a computer and sending it to a friend.

Table 4.2. Sequence game cards: "Cinderella"

> You start the game. Come to the center of the room and pantomime Cinderella doing chores around the house.

> The person before you has pantomimed Cinderella doing chores around the house.
>
> *You come to the center of the room and pantomime Cinderella asking her stepmother if she can go to the ball and being told no.*

> The person before you has pantomimed Cinderella asking her stepmother if she can go to the ball and being told no.
>
> *You come to the center of the room and pantomime Cinderella receiving a beautiful gown from the fairy godmother, trying it on, and showing that it fits.*

> The person before you has pantomimed Cinderella receiving a beautiful gown from the fairy godmother, trying it on, and showing that it fits.
>
> *You come to the center of the room and pantomime Cinderella putting on the glass slippers.*

> The person before you has pantomimed Cinderella putting on the glass slippers.
>
> *You come to the center of the room and pantomime Cinderella getting into a fine coach and riding to the ball.*

> The person before you has pantomimed Cinderella getting into a fine coach and riding to the ball.
>
> *You come to the center of the room and pantomime Cinderella dancing with the prince.*

> The person before you has pantomimed Cinderella dancing with the prince.
>
> *You come to the center of the room and pantomime Cinderella hearing the clock strike, running away, and losing her slipper.*

> The person before you has pantomimed Cinderella hearing the clock strike, running away, and losing her slipper.
>
> *You come to the center of the room and pantomime Cinderella hiding from the prince when he arrives at her cottage and watching through a keyhole while her stepsisters and stepmother try on the glass slipper.*

The person before you has pantomimed Cinderella hiding from the prince when he arrives at her cottage and watching through a keyhole while her stepsisters and stepmother try on the glass slipper.

You come to the center of the room and pantomime Cinderella trying on the slipper and showing that it fits.

The person before you has pantomimed Cinderella trying on the slipper and showing that it fits.

You come to the center of the room and pantomime Cinderella walking down the aisle at her wedding to the prince.

"Sounds of Rainbows"
Did you ever hear a rainbow
With its reds and yellows and blues?
Listen, after a rainstorm,
While the sun dries off your shoes.

Obviously, the movements suggested in each poem differ. Can players detect which poem is being performed if no recitation occurs?

GUIDELINES FOR PANTOMIMING PARAGRAPHS

- When narrating, pause for players to enact their ideas.
- Know the material well.
- Watch players and pace narration accordingly.
- Use expressive vocal quality.
- Play in unison, pairs or individually.

Pantomime Activity:
Pantomime Paragraphs
Pantomime paragraphs are simply a series of sentences, each with inherent action, unified by topic. They can be as short or as long as desired. Actions are performed as the leader narrates.

The following example demonstrates the importance of action in a pantomime paragraph.

Example: "Breakfast"

You have volunteered to make breakfast for your mother and father. Go to the refrigerator and take out juice. Walk to the table and pour juice into each of three small glasses. Return the juice to the refrigerator, and take out eggs and butter. Place these on the counter next to the stove. Now you select a frying pan from a hanging rack and place it on the stove. Get a knife from the silverware drawer. Use the knife to spread some butter in the frying pan. Turn on the burner. When the butter has melted, you crack three eggs into the pan. Be careful. You don't want any shells to get in the pan. While the eggs are cooking, throw away the shells. Return to the stove to check the eggs. They are ready to be turned, so you take a spatula from the utensil drawer next to the stove and flip the eggs. Place the spatula on the counter. The eggs are done now, so you turn off the stove. Call your parents to join you for a delicious breakfast.

Pantomime Activity:
Pantomime Stories

Just as pantomime sentences form pantomime paragraphs, pantomime stories are assembled from paragraphs. Stories can be original or come from published sources. If not originally designed for pantomime, they may require some editing. Large sections of descriptive narrative or dialogue do not lend themselves well to this type of activity because they provide little action. Pantomime, remember, requires showing or doing.

With narrative materials of any kind, it is helpful to read or tell the story prior to playing. This allows players to become familiar with the action and characters and to begin to form ideas related to interpretation. Keep in mind that work on pantomime paragraphs and stories generally improves with replaying.

REPLAYING MEANS DOING THE STORY AGAIN TO

- improve play;
- incorporate new ideas;
- cast new players.

Stories can focus on a single character that is played in unison, or they can have several characters requiring individual play (i.e., one person per role). Gender is unimportant, because in creative drama girls can play boys' roles and vice versa. In the following story, players could be given the choice of roles, or the leader might want to pair players and have one do each character. In either case, the example would then be played in unison. In a replay, roles could be switched, allowing players to experience both parts.

Example: "The Great Fishermen"

Mickey and Paul are excited. It is the first Saturday of the summer, and their parents are allowing them to go fishing alone. The brothers are determined to prove that they are two great fishermen.

Early in the morning, the boys wake up, wash, dress, and begin to pack their things. They gather together their fishing gear. Paul has to remind Mickey to take his good luck cap, and Mickey has to remind Paul to pack a first-aid kit. Finally, everything is ready.

The boys are so anxious to get started that they can barely eat their breakfast. But Mickey remembers that his mom told them to eat before leaving, and he doesn't want to disappoint her. He pours two big bowls of cereal, while Paul fixes them toast and pours two glasses of milk. The boys eat quickly. Then Paul writes a note to his parents that says "Gone fishing" and leaves it on the table. He and Mickey pick up their gear and head for the park.

Washington Park is only a half mile away from the boys' house, but it seems as if it is another world. The brothers soon find a comfortable spot not far from the water and set up all of their gear. They get their poles, lures, bait, and nets organized, then Paul casts his rod and leans against a log, waiting for his first catch of the day. Mickey has trouble baiting his hook, but eventually succeeds and puts his line in the water. He sits beside Paul. The boys close their eyes as the sun warms their faces. Soon both are asleep.

Suddenly, Paul feels a tug on his line. He awakens quickly and begins to pull in his catch. How surprised he is to see it is an old shoe! He takes the shoe off the hook, baits his line again, and throws it back into the water. Mickey wakes up, checks his line, and looks at Paul with disappointment. "I don't think we'll be having fish for lunch," he says. Paul agrees. Both boys decide to forget about fishing and they reel in their empty lines.

The water looks inviting, so the brothers decide that cooling off in the water will help them forget their lack of success as fishermen. They take off their shoes and socks and race each other to the water. Mickey and Paul play water games for hours. They have so much fun that they forget all about lunch. The games exhaust them, so they say little to each other as they get out of the water and stretch out in the sand, allowing the warm sun to dry them. Finally, Paul says, "We'd better go home now. Mom and Dad will be waiting for us."

It takes only a few minutes to gather everything together. Paul looks around and sees that Mickey has forgotten his good luck cap. He picks it up and puts it on his brother's head. The boys smile at each other. Even though they haven't caught any fish, they've had a great day. As they leave the park, each thinks about the summer days to come and how, no doubt, on one of them they will prove they are great fishermen.

ASSISTING THE PLAYERS: SIDECOACHING

The leader can give extra help to players by offering a descriptive narrative in the form of sentences or questions. This is called *sidecoaching*. Its purpose is to help players become more involved with the material by engaging their imaginations. Sidecoaching assists them in visualizing what will be depicted. As a guiding technique, it requires no verbal response from players, but produces more involved, detailed playing.

The leader should sidecoach when players have difficulty concentrating or becoming involved with the material. When students have trouble imagining or feel self-conscious and look at classmates,

either to imitate or distract them, sidecoaching subtly focuses their attention. It helps players commit to dramatic circumstances, and it can be done with the entire group or on an individual basis.

The leader should sidecoach as needed to help players produce detailed actions and make imaginative choices. When sidecoaching results in creative rather than imitative choices, players deserve praise. Examples of the technique follow, with sidecoaching commentary in parentheses.

Example 1: Literal Phrases
Come to a fork in the road. (What will you eat?)
Example 2: Pantomime Sentences
You are running in a marathon wearing shoes that are too tight for your feet. (How do your feet feel with each step you take?)
Show me how you would make the world's largest cake. (How tall is your cake? How wide is it? How will you frost and decorate it?)
Example 3: Pantomime Paragraph

You have volunteered to make breakfast for your mother and father. Go to the refrigerator and take out juice. Walk to the table and pour juice into each of three small glasses. (What kind of juice are you serving? Maybe some of you will serve pineapple juice while others will serve orange juice. There are many different kinds of juices. What is your favorite?) Return the juice to the refrigerator, and take out eggs and butter. (Be careful carrying the eggs.) Place these on the counter next to the stove. Now you select a frying pan from a hanging rack and place it on the stove. (How heavy is your frying pan?) Get a knife from the silverware drawer. Use the knife to spread some butter in the frying pan. Turn on the burner. (What kind of stove are you using? I see that some are using gas stoves and some are using electric stoves.) When the butter has melted, you crack three eggs into the pan. Be careful. You don't want any shells to get in the pan. (That wouldn't taste good.) While the eggs are cooking, throw away the shells. Return to the stove to check the eggs. They are ready to be turned, so you take a spatula from the utensil drawer next to the stove and flip the eggs. (You're being so careful. You don't want to break the yolks.) Place the spatula on the counter. The eggs are done now, so you turn off the stove. (How do they look? How do they smell?) Call your parents to join you for a delicious breakfast.

When the leader sees that only one player is not involved in the activity, sidecoaching can be given on an individual basis. The leader stands beside the player and quietly sidecoaches. Whether it is done for unison play or for an individual, players already involved in the activity hardly notice the assistance. It seems to help those who need it and is blocked out by those who don't.

In either application, open-ended questions are recommended. An open-ended question is one that requires more than just a yes or no answer. (Those requiring yes or no answers are called *closed questions*.) In the creative process, open-ended questions are preferred for stimulating imagination and producing divergent and in-depth thinking. Open-ended questions produce the best creative results.

RECOMMENDED LISTENING AND MOVEMENT REPERTORY

Highly Rhythmic Music

Leonard Bernstein	*West Side Story*, "Cool"
Johannes Brahms	Symphony no. 1 in C Minor, first movement
Dave Brubeck	*Take Five*, "Rondo à la Turk"
Aaron Copland	*Rodeo*
Claude Debussy	*Children's Corner* Suite: "Golliwogg's Cakewalk"
Paul Dukas	*The Sorcerer's Apprentice*
George Gershwin	*Preludes*
	Rhapsody in Blue
Morton Gould	*American Salute*
Zoltán Kodály	*Háry János* Suite
Nikolai Rimske Korsakov	*Scheherezade*
Modest Mussorgsky	*Pictures at an Exhibition*
Camille Saint-Saëns	*Carnival of Animals*
Bedřich Smetana	*The Moldau*
Igor Stravinsky	*Pétrouchka*
	The Rite of Spring
	A Soldier's Tale

Music with Repetition

Johann Sebastian Bach	*Well Tempered Clavier*
Ludwig van Beethoven	Symphony no. 5 in C Minor, first movement
	Für Elise
Aaron Copland	*Fanfare for the Common Man*
	Appalachian Spring, "Simple Gifts"
Maurice Ravel	*Bolero*
Erik Satie	*Gymnopédies*
Ralph Vaughan Williams	*Fantasia on Greensleeves*

Music with Varying Tempos

Samuel Barber	Adagio for Strings
Bela Bartók	String Quartet, second movement
Frédéric Chopin	Waltz in D-flat Major, op. 64 (*Minute*)
Claude Debussy	*La mer*
George Gershwin	*An American in Paris*

Edvard Grieg	*Peer Gynt* Suite: "In the Hall of the Mountain King"
Arthur Honegger	*Pacific 231*
Charles Ives	*Variations of "America"*
Wolfgang Amadeus Mozart	Symphony no. 40 in G Minor, K. 550
	Piano Variations on "Ah, vous dirai-je, Maman" ("Twinkle, Twinkle, Little Star")
Modest Mussorgsky	*Night on Bald Mountain*
Gioacchino Rossini	Overture to *William Tell*
Richard Strauss	*Till Eulenspiegel*
Peter I. Tchaikovsky	*Nutcracker* Suite
	1812 Overture
Virgil Thomson	Suite from "The River"
Ralph Vaughan Williams	Overture to *The Wasps*

Music with Varying Dynamics

Ludwig van Beethoven	*Moonlight* Sonata
	Appassionata Sonata
Georges Bizet	*Carmen* Suite no. 1
Alexander Borodin	*Polovetsian Dances*
Claude Debussy	*Pelléas et Mélisande*
	Sicilienne
Gabriel Urbain Fauré	*Claire de lune*
Claude Debussy	*Claire de lune*
Sergei Prokofiev	*Lieutenant Kije* Suite
Ralph Vaughan Williams	*The Lark Ascending*

SAMPLE LESSON, CHAPTER 4

LESSON OVERVIEW: This lesson integrates creative drama and music activities with several areas of science. Players will learn about rain forests, animals, and insects through pantomime and creative movement activities.

RECOMMENDED GRADE: 5

CONTENT AREAS: drama/theatre, music, and science

INSTRUCTIONAL OBJECTIVES:

- Players will recognize that the natural world can be better understood through careful observation. (Science)
- Players will demonstrate the use of concentration, sensory awareness, imagination, and physical control of artistic choices. (Drama/theatre)
- Players will analyze the presence of elements of music in aural examples and respond through purposeful movement to selected music events. (Music)

LENGTH OF LESSON: thirty-five to forty-five minutes

ACTIVITIES AND PROCEDURES:

Preparation: Show students pictures or videos of the living creatures in the activities that follow. Discuss their features, their habitats, and other interesting facts.

Pantomime Poem: "The Ant and the Cricket," by Anonymous

Pair the players and ask them to pantomime the poem as the leader narrates it. One person should play the ant and the other the cricket. It is a good idea to read the poem aloud once before playing. Give students the opportunity to switch roles and replay.

After playing, discuss the moral. Encourage players to consider the importance of the seasons in each character's life.

"The Ant and the Cricket"
By Anonymous
A silly young cricket, accustomed to sing
Through the warm, sunny months of
    gay summer and spring,
Began to complain, when he found
    that at home
His cupboard was empty and winter
    was come.
Not a crumb to be found
On the snow-covered ground;

Not a flower could he see
Not a leaf on a tree.

"Oh, what will become," says the
    cricket, "of me?"
At last by starvation and famine made
    bold,
All dripping with wet and all trembling
    with cold,
Away he set off to a miserly ant
To see if, to keep him alive, he would
    grant
Him shelter from rain.
A mouthful of grain
He wished only to borrow,
He'd repay it to-morrow;
If not helped, he must die of starvation
    and sorrow.

Says the ant to the cricket: "I'm your
    servant and friend,
But we ants never borrow, we ants
    never lend.
Pray tell me, dear sir, did you lay
    nothing by
When the weather was warm?" Said
    the cricket, "Not I.
My heart was so light
That I sang day and night,
For all nature looked gay."
"You sang, sir, you say?
Go then," said the ant, "and sing
    winter away."

Thus ending, he hastily lifted the
    wicket
And out of the door turned the poor
    little cricket.
Though this is a fable, the moral is
    good—
If you live without work, you must live
    without
Food.[1]

Creative Movement:
Carnival of Animals
Use a narrated version of the *Carnival
of Animals* for this activity. Composer
Camille Saint-Saëns was a famous French

composer who gave his first piano recital
in Paris before he was five years old. He
composed his first composition at age
six. He won many prizes for his compositions. "Carnival" is a wonderful way to
explore Saint-Saëns' sense of humor, as
he portrays the personality of each animal
through musical characteristics.

The goal of this activity is to help players connect certain musical characteristics
with appropriate movements. "Appropriate" does not necessarily mean exact
mimicking. Rather, appropriate creativity
involves expressing the characteristics as
felt in the music. Focusing on the music in-
forms and inspires expressive movement.

The composition has thirteen sections,
each depicting a different animal. The
leader should select only two or three
sections for the first listening, then ask the
players to determine the overall mood or
soundscape as they try to identify the animal. A second listening then challenges
the players to compare and contrast the
animals. The leader draws the players' attention to the rhythm, mood, dynamics,
and **style** of the music. On the third time
through the players, having had at least
two opportunities to listen, plan their
creative movements to the music.

The sample queries below will help
the leader stimulate creative thinking
through open-ended questions for several of the thirteen sections. During this
sample lesson, expect the players to create
movement for only one or two animals.

1. Lions
   What animal might be portrayed
   in the music? Why do you think
   so? How can we convey that we
   are "kings" of the forest? Why do
   you think this animal is first in the
   carnival? How can you demonstrate this animal's size? How does
   the music encourage you to strut,

march, whimper, or slink around? What elements of the music help portray the lions? (Rhythm, melody, harmony, form, dynamics, tempo, instrumentation)

2. Chickens
How do you know that there is more than one animal in this section? What are these animals doing? How can you demonstrate their size? Where are they in space? How can you express the rhythm of the chickens' movements?

3. Donkeys
Something in the music "gives away" what animal is in this section of the carnival. What is it? How do you know that this animal is climbing and descending? How might you move to portray the tempo of this animal?

4. Tortoises
Don't be fooled by some distracting action in this section. Listen for the low string melody and decide if this animal is a slow or fast mover. How do you know that this animal is one that lives close to the ground? How can your movements show this?

5. Fish
What instruments give you the feeling that you are swimming? How do you move smoothly through water? At what tempo are you swimming? How can your face help show fish movements?

6. Kangaroos
What animal is portrayed in this section? What element in the music gave you the biggest clue? How big is the kangaroo? How big are the jumps? How many jumps are appropriate?

7. Cuckoo Bird
Before this animal makes a sound, you are in a huge, thick, dark forest. Feel the presence. How big are you? How does the animal sound in comparison to the forest? Look

around—you are the only one moving. Show how this makes you feel.

Narrative Pantomime Paragraph: "A Walk in the Rain Forest"

Players can apply sensory awareness and imagination to this pantomime paragraph.

"A Walk in the Rain Forest"
You are exploring a rain forest in the Northern Territory of Australia. You stand at the entrance to the path and feel the hot sun on your face. You wipe the sweat from your brow with your hand. You walk a few steps along the sandy path and enter the rain forest proper. The temperature immediately feels cooler. You stop along the path, look down, and see a funnel-shaped trap in the sand. You kneel down and use your finger to knock a little sand down the side of the funnel. You see movement and know that a tiger ant is hiding in a trap that he has made within the funnel. You stand and continue down the path. It changes from sand to bark. You listen to the crunch, crunch beneath your feet as you walk. You stop by a plant, pick some of its small leaves, crush them in your hand, and raise your hand to your nose. Breathe deeply. Your smile shows how much you enjoy the scent of the fresh mint leaves. Let them fall through your fingers and onto the ground. Continue walking along the path until you come to a large banyan tree. It has grown from one side of the path to the other. You walk all around the tree, examining it carefully. You notice that the bark has a shape like a mushroom and know that this odd shape has been created by feral pigs scratching their backs against the tree. You decide to imitate the feral pigs and, crouching near the bark, wiggle from side to side as you scratch your back against the banyan tree. Laughing

to yourself, you start walking. You stop laughing when you see beautiful butterflies fluttering past. You stop, capture one in your hands, and then open your hands and release it. You watch it fly away. You move down the path until you come to water. You know it is pure, fresh, and cold. Kneel down at the bank and scoop the water with your cupped hands. Splash some on your face. Now it is time to go back. Stand and start walking up the path. Take a big step over a log that lies across the path. Walk a few more steps and then stop. You see an egret. Stand perfectly still and watch the bird. Be quiet so that you don't startle the beautiful white creature. After a few moments, you hear a noise. Look up. Many birds are flying overhead. Shade your eyes with your hands as you watch them fly toward the sun that filters through the treetops. It's time to go, so you reluctantly climb the small upgrade that takes you back to your all-terrain vehicle. As you leave the path and emerge again into bright sunlight, you think about how cool and peaceful the rain forest is. You wave a silent good-bye to all of nature's creatures residing in the rain forest.

ASSESSMENT: Complete the rubric shown in table 4.3.

NOTE

1. Anonymous. "The Ant and the Cricket," at www.apples4theteacher.com/holidays/winter/poems-rhymes/the-ant-and-the-cricket.html.

Table 4.3. Rubric for Sample Lesson

	Yes	No	In part
Players have incorporated their knowledge of animals and insects into their pantomiming and creative movement.			
Players have used physical skills to create inhabitants of the natural world.			
Players have used imagination, sensory awareness, and concentration to effect believable characterizations.			

CHAPTER 5

Building Blocks for Creative Choices

Surprises can be fun. In creative drama and music, not knowing what comes next can produce rewards. Introducing improvisational experiences challenges players to integrate and apply a number of skills. In this chapter, activities focus on vocal and physical skills and are designed to facilitate listening, teamwork, and independent thinking. They encourage and support spontaneity in creative drama and music. Players can demonstrate their creativity and experience positive personal growth as artistic elements and abilities start to come together.

Players may signal the leader that they are ready to integrate skills in more difficult and less structured activities. For example, players engaged in pantomime activities may begin to use sounds. If these sounds don't contribute to the action, participants should be reminded that pantomime is silent. If, however, sounds seem to be a natural outgrowth of the action, such as when a player pantomiming a puppy barks or one playing a baby says "Mama," these verbal responses may be signs of involvement indicating readiness for dialogue. Once players demonstrate an ability to concentrate, to show confidence in pantomime, and to use the body to communicate, they are ready for activities that develop vocal techniques, focus on characterization, and foster quick thinking and cooperation.

Activities in this chapter observe the sequences from simple to complex and teacher directed to student directed. The overarching goal is to nurture spontaneity and creative expression through individual and group experiences.

CREATIVE CHOICES IN MUSIC: ENSEMBLE SINGING (LOWER/UPPER LEVELS)

Some of the most satisfying musical experiences occur during group singing sessions. All players can improve their singing skills with modest guidance from the leader and have more fun in doing so. Whether players are singing a simple camp song or a multiverse folk ballad, there are a few guidelines that can help in effective performance.

In ensemble work, the goal is for the players to blend their voices. This requires sensitivity to starting and ending together; staying together at the same tempo; singing on the correct pitch; and making sure the volume level is desirable. Players should be encouraged to sing freely, but fit into the choral sound. Leaders can help keep the ensemble singing well by giving cues through conducting.

Some leaders may lack the ability to sing on pitch and accurately in rhythm. We recommend that insecure singers use instruments (piano, resonator bells) or recordings to model correct pitches and rhythms.

The leader needs to establish the starting time and opening pitch so that everyone begins singing together and in tune. Even if an instrument or recording is used to teach songs, it is necessary to guide players so they start on the same pitch and at the same time. To establish the tempo and entrance point involves rhythmic preparation. The leader may conduct or count preparatory beats. Young players can follow best when the leader both conducts and counts beats.

Rhythmic Preparation
Leaders may wish to use conducting patterns to lead the ensemble. In printed music, time signature will indicate the metric pattern. For songs in duple meter (often designated by a 2/4 or 6/8 time signature), two major beats are gestured. Triple meter (often designated by a 3/4 time signature) will contain three gestures. For songs in 4/4, or common time (C), four beats are contained in the pattern. The patterns in figure 5.1 will be helpful for conducting songs in these respective meters. (The leader may wish to refer to the discussion of time signatures in chapter 2 to review the sense of beats in metric patterns.)

If the upper number of the time signature is divisible by two, it calls for a duple or quadruple conducting pattern. If the lower number is a 4, the quarter note ($\quarternote$) will receive one beat.

These conducting patterns should be practiced so that the leader feels familiar and comfortable with them when leading songs. The patterns may also be taught to advanced players who may, in turn, serve as student conductors.

Pitch Preparation
It is always preferable for the leader to sing or hum the starting pitch of a song. Some leaders who are not vocally confident, however, may use an instrument to play the tone. If that is the case, it is recommended that all players echo the starting pitch once it is given. With very young players who are marginal listeners, the leader may remind them to listen carefully and try (again) to match the pitch.

If the leader does not have an instrument such as a pitch pipe or xylophone to play the starting pitch, the song should be quietly rehearsed before group singing. This will ensure that the song is pitched

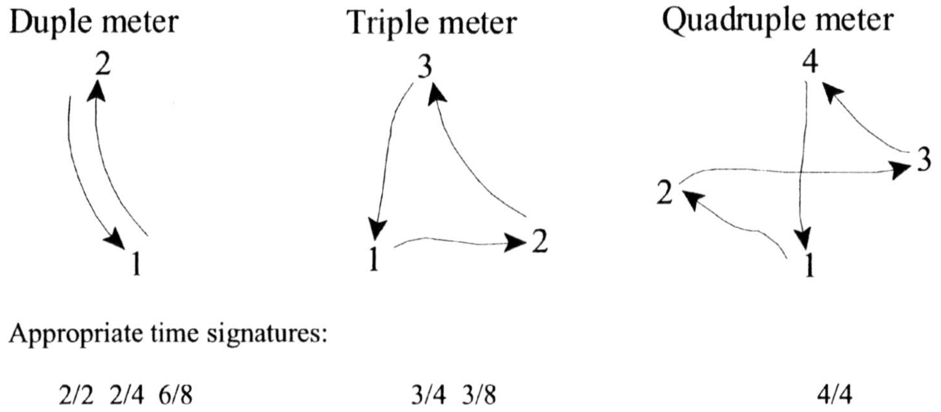

Duple meter   Triple meter   Quadruple meter

Appropriate time signatures:

2/2 2/4 6/8   3/4 3/8   4/4

Figure 5.1

in a comfortable range: not too low or too high.

Selecting Songs

What are the characteristics of a good song? One rule of thumb is that if the leader appreciates the song, the players will likely enjoy it, too. Songs that appeal to children generally have some rhythmic interest, are pitched within a comfortable singing range, and have suitable content. Generally, elementary-age learners can sing songs pitched within the C scale. If the majority of the pitches fall within the range shown in figure 5.2, most children will be able to sing them.

Many songs have pitches slightly above and below this range. Older players have more expanded singing ranges, and they are able to sing these songs comfortably. Songs with suitable ranges may be found in chapter 2. After selecting songs for players to sing, the leader should practice starting, for confidence with the conducting pattern and pitch preparation.

Figure 5.2

ENSEMBLE PLAYING IN DRAMA (UPPER/LOWER LEVELS)

In creative drama, an *ensemble* is a group that works together. No one player is more important than another. There is no distinction made between starring and supporting roles. Ensemble playing means not working for individual glory or recognition and being respectful of partners' abilities. Players are concerned with give and take. They must be listening, reacting to, and concentrating on each other. They must be sharing the process in order to successfully express ideas. No matter how simple or complex the tasks, players work together for the common artistic good.

Ensemble playing should be a natural outgrowth of work in creative drama and music. It requires acknowledging work that is well done; helping those who are having difficulty; cooperating; and learning to follow the natural course of an activity. Teamwork, rather than an imposition of ideas, is the expectation. A leader's positive reinforcement is important here, as is the players' desire to succeed. Ensemble playing results when players and leader value each other's input and guidance.

The following activities are designed to build ensemble. The building blocks here relate to players' interdependency. Individual contributions are layered, producing the architecture for ensemble.

Ensemble Improvisation Activity: Hello—Theme and Variations

This activity explores the potential of the speaking voice for a variety of sound effects. Players will enjoy taking a simple greeting word, such as *hello*, and varying the word by voicing it with different expressions such as surprise, exhaustion, questioning, and so forth. Players may experiment with different volume levels (dynamics), from a solo secret to a loud declamatory chorus.

Older players can be asked to think of different ways to convey greetings other than through the word *hello*. Players might suggest greetings in foreign languages, such as *hola*, *jamba*, or other variations.

The leader should use this as an opportunity to introduce the musical form of theme and variations. Composers often state a theme and then vary it. The composition has a certain amount of unity with the thematic variations, but it does not consist of redundant repetition.

Ensemble Activity: How Can You Say . . . ?

Similar to the previous activity and designed to target vocal expressiveness, this circle game requires players to think of as many different ways as possible to say a particular word, phrase, or sentence. Ways of changing delivery include raising or lowering pitch or volume, accenting different syllables, and changing punctuation. The leader begins with a word, phrase, or sentence, using a delivery that is relatively neutral so as not to influence other interpretations. Each player repeats what the leader has said. No one, however, can repeat a vocal inflection. Should this happen, the leader should acknowledge that the interpretation has been used previously and ask the player to try again.

Suggested lines follow. Of course, the leader and players will be able to add many others to this list. At the activity's conclusion, pointing out that *how* something is said is just as important as *what* is said will help players realize the importance of vocal expression. What a person is thinking and feeling will affect speaking and the development of believable characterizations. **Subtext** (the thoughts and emotions underlying the dialogue) will likely influence delivery.

Example:

(The italicized words are accented.)

Leader: I've never seen him before.

Player 1: *I've* never seen him before.

Player 2: I've *never* seen him before.

Player 3: I've never *seen* him before!

Player 4: I've never seen *him* before?

Player 5: I've never seen him *before.*

Other sentences that work well include the following:

I don't care.
Don't.
I like you.
Come here.
I don't believe it.
Why not?
What are you doing?

Ensemble Improvisation Activity: Word Painting with the Voice

Another exercise in vocal improvisation involves vocabulary building. The idea here is to perform the word with added meaning. Word painting involves articulating the term's meaning or mood with special vocal effects. For example, the word *sizzle* can be vocally performed to convey the sounds of bacon sizzling through emphasis on the *s* and *z* sounds. The following words have expressive potential:

magic	gooey	cold
good morning!	pitter patter	ding dong
bueno	nebulous	plop
whisper	gritty	thunderstorms
ticktock	plead	freaky
spooky	pop	slick
ogre	stoic	war
weird	fizzle	fragile
hola	pronto	google
tweet		

Players can control many musical elements in their word painting. This is accomplished if they control the dynamics, tempo, pitch, accents, and articulation, as well as special effects such as hissing or exaggerating consonants.

CIRCLE GAMES
(LOWER/UPPER LEVELS)

Circle games emphasize listening and concentration. Players stand or sit in a circle. These activities require little or no movement and can be used to balance pacing in a session. Circle games challenge the intellect, develop the voice, and require players to stay focused. Results are often pleasantly unpredictable.

Circle Activity: Buzz Game

In this activity, the leader whispers a word, phrase, or sentence to a player, who then whispers it to the next player, and so on around the circle until everyone has heard it. Each player may only whisper once; the message cannot be repeated for clarification. After hearing it, the last player states the message. If communication has been clear, the word, phrase, or sentence will match the original. If it is different, which is common, a nonjudgmental discussion can center on communication breakdown and how it happened. The goal of this activity is to begin and end with the same message. While the group can enjoy sharing laughter resulting from humorous confusion, this should not overshadow the "Buzz Game's" true purpose.

Players may know this exercise from experiences unrelated to creative drama. Within a dramatic context, however, it encourages careful pronunciation, articulation, delivery, and listening. Different messages can be used for replaying.

Example:

Original message: My dog is brown and black.

The breakdown: My hog was drowned out back.

Circle Activity: Vocal Hide and Seek

Even young players have success in being vocal detectives during this game. In "Vocal Hide and Seek," one player is blindfolded and placed in the middle of a circle. The blindfolded player points to another player, who says:

Eeany, meany, miney, mo,
Say my name or 'round we go.

The blindfolded player must identify the speaker by his or her voice. If the player is not identified, the circle moves around a few steps. If the voice is identified correctly, the speaking player becomes the new voice "investigator."

For additional challenge, the players improvise on their speaking voices, that is, incorporating some distortions or changes. The clever disguises will challenge players of all ages.

CHORAL READING
(UPPER/LOWER LEVELS)

Choral reading is musical speech. It involves speaking with a sense of rhythm, **melody**, harmony, form, tone color (vocal quality), and dynamics. Choral reading brings more meaning to text through exaggerated expressiveness. Players will vary the tempo, dynamics, pitch level, and articulation of their speech. The result is an interpretive performance rather than mere recitation by a group of speakers.

To help players determine how to perform a poem or text, a certain amount of analysis must precede choral-reading performance. First, players must have an adequate amount of time to study the poem or text. Second, it is advisable for each player to either have a copy of the reading or keep in sight a large copy that is projected on a chart or overhead screen.

Once some choral performance decisions have been made, the player or leader can mark the copy appropriately. To illustrate, a line of a poem might become gradually softer, and the players would note that directly on the copy.

Third, the leader can foster creativity among the players through strategic questioning. The text of the material usually contains hints or clues as to how the reading might be enhanced. Finally, not every poem or text will lend itself to choral treatment, and the leader should review the questions in tables 5.1–5.6 as part of the selection process. It may be appropriate to focus on one musical quality per poem until players are experienced with all elements of music.

Tables 5.1–5.6 list some sample questions, organized around musical elements that might be part of the performance. The questions—both open and closed—are framed for direct use with children.

Study the poem "The Bike Ride," for choral reading potential:

"The Bike Ride"
Push, push, pump, pump,
Road is pocked with pit and bump.
Gears spin, click, tick,
Riding faster. Quick, quick, quick!
Knees rise, fall, bend,
Power to the pedals send.
Wind gusts. I thrust,
Bursting through on wheels I trust!

Note that the content lends itself naturally to sound effects and expressive interpretation. The leader should select just a few aspects of the poem for analysis ahead of time, and focus on exploring them for imaginative results. To approach the process creatively, it is recommended that the leader first read the poem and discuss its meaning. This will foster richer choices.

Suggested questions for preparing the above poem for choral reading might include the following:

1. Should we recite the poem as a chorus in unison or arrange parts for smaller groups and solos?

Table 5.1. Rhythm

1. How does this poem (quotation, story) make you feel?
2. Does it have a sense of movement as I read it?
3. Can you move your hands or feet to the movement of the line?
4. Can you feel a beat as I read it?
5. Do you notice any accents (sudden emphasis or stress) in the first stanza?
6. How fast or slow should this poem be read? Shall we speed up (**accelerando**) or slow down (**ritardando**) at any point?
7. Do you feel beats moving in a metric (duple or triple) pattern in each line?

Table 5.2. Melody

1. What is the mood of this poem?
2. Would it be more appropriate to use high voices or low voices?
3. Are there lines in which one voice might move upward or downward for **melodic direction**?
4. Can we word paint any special or important words?
   How can special parts be emphasized with melodic voices?
5. Where do you feel phrases?
   Shall we take a pause or breath at any particular time?
   How can we show a pause with our voices?

Table 5.3. Harmony/texture

1. What part of the poem should be recited by everyone (in unison)?
2. Are there sections that would be more effective if performed solo, or by a duet, trio, or small ensemble?
3. Shall we all start together, or are there places that call for staggered entrances or an echo technique?
4. Should we have some sounds accompany the reading?
   Should they be voices, found/environmental sounds, or instruments?
5. What type of musical harmony (**consonance** or **dissonance**) helps set the mood?

Table 5.4. Form

1. Can you feel definite sections or parts in this poem?
   How can we set them apart and make them sound like sections?
2. Is there any unity throughout the poem?
   How can we perform that unity in our voices or accompaniment?
3. Is there any contrast?
   How can we perform that contrast in our voices or accompaniment?
4. How can we provide some unity to this poem?
5. How will we know when to start, pause, and end together?

Table 5.5. Tone Color

1. What sounds (vocal, body, instrument, or found) best describe what is happening in the poem?
2. Where can we find the sounds (body sounds, found sounds, instruments, recorded music, etc.)?
3. How shall we articulate these sounds—as smooth or detached (short, separated, and choppy)?
4. Will our sounds imitate something real or create new, imaginative effects?
5. Do we want a sound to recur at the suggestion of a special person, thing, or event (leitmotif idea)?
6. Where can we effectively use silence in the poem?

Table 5.6. Dynamics

1. How loud or soft should this performance be?
2. Is there any place where we should use gradually increasing dynamics or decreasing dynamics?
3. How loud should the accompaniment be?

---

2. What type of accompanying sounds will help tell this story? Are body sounds appropriate? Found sounds? Vocal sounds? Instruments? Why or why not?

3. When the leader reads the poem the first time, can the players feel the beat? How many beats are sensed in each line?

4. Does the poem suggest a particular speed? Should it change?

For the first experience, the leader should help players decide if the poem should be read as a chorus (in unison); as a series of soloists; or as a combination of choral ensemble and soloists. Then the leader may invite the group to decide what type of accompaniment is appropriate. Next, are there any rhythmic, melodic, dynamic, or sound effect features that could enhance the performance? The leader should select just a few questions for discussion from tables 5.1–5.6, but allow the players to make the musical choices—even if they do not seem to be the most artistic. During a critique, the group will likely come to reassess unwise choices and strive to make better ones.

CHARACTERIZATION (UPPER/LOWER LEVELS)

Characters are those people, animals, or personified objects that interact in a story. Interest and meaning are created by their actions and reactions and by their relationships. The tools of **characterization** are the voice and the body. Players must find the correct posture, appearance, vocal tones, inflection, and personal rhythm to interpret a particular character truthfully and multidimensionally; those that are only one-dimensional are *caricatures.*

In some characterization activities, the player is called upon to make quick decisions and to find traits or images that are easily recognized. These choices help in understanding the foundation upon which characterization is based, and most often produce simple rather than complex interpretations. Once players are confident and successful with these beginning experiences, they can look to more serious portrayals in such complex activities as story creation and story dramatization.

One key assessment question becomes, "Is the behavior *believable?*" In other words, would the character think and speak this way, and would the character perform these actions? While recognizing that believability and reality are not synonymous terms and should not

CHARACTERIZATION QUESTIONS

- How is this character like me?
- How is this character unlike me?
- What does the character say about him- or herself?
- What do others say about the character?
- How does the author describe the character?
- What do the character's actions reveal?

be confused, a player should still strive to create a character (even a unicorn, wizard, princess, or frog) who is credible. Interpretation should be truthful for a particular character within the life of the story.

Characterization Activity: Radio Sound Bites

A simple characterization activity that emphasizes the voice is "Radio Sound Bites." This activity is based upon the idea of changing radio stations so that programs overlap. Players are cast and scripts distributed to those doing roles. After the playing, all members of the group may be given a copy of the script for their personal enjoyment, but limited distribution for play ensures listening rather than reading. When the radio is turned "on," cues should be picked up quickly so that the lines of different characters merge, often producing humorous results.

Here are several hints that can help ensure success with this activity: First, allow adequate time for the preparation of scripts. In developing a "Radio Sound Bites" session, the leader begins with the idea that each player is giving a **monologue**, and that these monologues are broken up by the imaginary changing of

- They provide training in using voice for characterization.
- Using short phrases alleviates the pressure slow readers may feel when reading long passages aloud.
- Imaginations can be stimulated as players envision themselves working at a radio station.
- Listening and concentration are developed through prompt response to cues.

stations. This may necessitate the elimination of some words, but the premise remains that each character is delivering a coherent story, interview, or report, and lines should be written that way. Radio, television, magazines, or newspapers should help in creating the proper format. If the players enjoy the "Radio Sound Bites" activity, the leader might encourage them to create their own scripts as part of a lesson on media.

Example:

Teacher: Long ago, when people wished to communicate, they used . . .

Sports Announcer: . . . a penalty flag. That will put the ball on the 30-yard line and . . .

Radio DJ: . . . really light up the charts. This new record by the . . .

Farm Announcer: . . . cattle growers report a decline in livestock production that will effect . . .

Radio DJ: . . . this week's top of the charts. Holding the top spot for the third week in a row is . . .

Teacher: . . . the Morse Code. This system of dots and dashes . . .

Farm Announcer: . . . is guaranteed to produce bigger yields without causing . . .

Sports Announcer: . . . an interception. This game has been marred by a series of careless plays which . . .

Teacher: . . . made printed material available to the general population. The printing press also . . .

Radio DJ: . . . has a mellow sound. Couples will be dancing to this one for a long time to come. So listen with someone special and . . .

Sports Announcer: . . . punt. The team was unable to make a first down and will now . . .

Teacher: . . . develop more sophisticated means of communication. In the Old West, the telegraph poles became . . .

Farm Announcer: . . . a new idea in crop rotation. In an effort to retain top-soil . . .

Sports Announcer: . . . the specialty team has come onto the field. They'll try to . . .

Radio DJ: . . . sing your favorite song . . .

Farm Announcer: . . . as long as hog prices remain stable.

*Characterization Activity:
Radio Sound Bites Variation*
More advanced players can substitute television for radio. Groups of players form the casts of various television shows, and each group occupies its own playing space. An example would be a crime scene investigation show, a reality show, and a newscast. Each group is numbered, and players create the action for their particular show. The leader calls a group number. As one group freezes, a new group begins. Numbers are called in random order, and scenes are viewed as they would be when changing television channels.

Example:

    Leader: Group 1 begin.

    (They play.)

        Freeze. Group 3 begin.

    (They play.)

        Freeze. Group 2 begin.

    (They play.)

        Freeze. Group 1.

    (They play.)

        Freeze. Group 2.

    (They play.)

Characterization Activity:
Autobiographies

For autobiographies and similar exercises, a picture file is a useful resource. Pictures from magazines, books, the Internet, and newspapers, as well as photographs, can inspire characterizations. Favorite pictures should be preserved through lamination.

For autobiographies, players select pictures that interest them and then envision themselves as the people depicted. The leader should give sufficient time for studying pictures and imagining life stories. Players can then write or orally relate the autobiographies for their selected characters. If the activity is done orally, the player should use a voice that suits the character.

Example (based on a picture of an old man):

> I have worked hard all of my life. When I was a little boy in England, I helped my father in his store. He was a chemist, which is the same as being a pharmacist in the United States. During the big war, I was a soldier. I met an American nurse and married her. When the war ended, we came to this country to raise our family. I worked in an auto plant until a few years ago. Now I am retired and a widower. My children and grandchildren come to visit me, but I am still very lonely.

Characterization Activity:
Autobiographies Variation

Rather than using pictures to inspire characterization, the leader might substitute costume pieces, hats, or **props**. The players would then have to create their autobiographies based on who might wear or use the item.

Characterization Activity:
Man-in-the-Street Interviews

This is a natural extension of autobiographies. The leader provides minimal information about the circumstances. Inspired by photographs, costumes, props, or imagination, several players create characters who have witnessed an event such as an auto accident or a robbery. They take their place at the scene. Then the leader acting **in role**, or another player, enters as a reporter, police officer, or similar figure who conducts interviews, with players responding in character.

Those interviewed in the following example are a rich lady and a little boy, although any combination is possible. The leader plays in role as a reporter, and the event is a car accident that the characters have witnessed.

Example:

> Leader: Tell me, madam, did you see what happened?
>
> Rich Lady: Well, it was really awful. I was on my way to the jewelry store when the car in front of me ran into a telephone pole. This will back up traffic for hours, and I really must get to the store to pick up my diamond rings.
>
> (Exits.)
>
> Leader: Thank you. Little boy, what did you see?
>
> Little Boy: I was playing with my ball when the lady in the blue car did a really

dumb thing. She drove right into that telephone pole.

Leader: Was she hurt?

Little Boy: I don't know, but the noise sure scared me. Can I go now?

Leader: Thank you for your description.

GROUP STORY BUILDING (LOWER/UPPER LEVELS)

In group story building in creative drama, players spontaneously create and build content. The results can be realistic or fanciful. The stories help prepare players for more complex story work.

Among the techniques for building stories are the continuing story and "Good News/Bad News." These require players to listen carefully in order to form complete works.

Group Story Activity:
The Continuing Story

The leader starts to tell an original story, stopping at any point, even in mid-sentence. The player next to the leader must continue the story without repeating words or adding responses such as "uh" or "let's see." To illustrate, suppose the leader has concluded with "and then . . ." The next player cannot say, "And then he . . ." Starting with a new word, that player continues and then breaks the story for the next person. Players who repeat words or who cannot think of anything to say are eliminated, and the next person continues. The last player concludes the story.

The continuing story is an enjoyable way to foster quick thinking. The nature of the activity makes it difficult to plan in advance, as players must respond to story events as they unfold. Additions may be brief at first but will become longer as players gain experience. Encourage them

to contribute imaginative complications to the plot. That is what makes this activity fun!

Example 1: "The Audition"

Leader: The announcement was posted on a school bulletin board. It said that the local theatre was looking for young actors to be in a production of *Peter Pan*. Auditions would be held at the theatre on Monday evening, and interested students should attend.

Player 1: Cameron thought that sounded like fun. He wanted to be in a play. Maybe he could become famous!

Player 2: When Cameron asked his parents to take him to the audition, however, his father said that he had to work that evening. Cameron's mother said that she thought he already had too many after school activities and really did not have time to be in a play.

Player 3: Cameron was disappointed. "What if," he asked his parents, "I find another ride to the theatre and I give up an after school activity? Then could I audition?"

Player 4: Cameron's parents thought for a moment. "That seems reasonable," his father said. "All right," his mother said, "but if you are cast you will need to give up something else."

Player 5: Cameron called his friend Robert and explained the situation. "My mom is taking me," said Robert. "You can come with us."

Player 6: "Great!" said Cameron. "Maybe we will both become famous!"

Continuing stories are challenging and more fun if, rather than going around the circle in a predictable order, the order is random. This makes the activity more student directed. It also emphasizes listening and concentration, while building excitement.

The second example shows how content areas, in this case math, can be integrated into the story. It also illustrates how the activity is played.

Example 2: "The Fun Fair"

Leader: We were having a fun fair to mark the end of the school year. Two students, Pat and Chris, decided to have a contest of their own. They wanted to see which one of them could win more points and get a bigger prize. Pat said, "Let's start at the ring-toss game. I'm good at that." When they played . . .

Player 1: Pat, however, was not very good at tossing the rings. Pat only won a ticket worth five points. "My turn," said Chris, and . . .

Player 2: Chris tossed the rings. They all landed successfully. Chris received a ticket worth ten points. Next, they . . .

Player 3: They . . .

Leader: Stop. (Because the player repeated a word, she is eliminated.)

Player 4: . . . went to the goldfish game. Chris loved this game.

Player 5: Uh . . .

Leader: Stop. (Because the player did not begin by saying a word, he is eliminated.)

Player 6: Chris threw Ping-Pong balls into three of the five fish bowls that were set up and got a ticket worth five points.

Player 7: Pat threw Ping-Pong balls into all five fish bowls. Pat received a ticket worth ten points.

Player 8: "Let's get our prizes," the friends said as they . . .

Player 9: (Cannot think of an answer and is eliminated.)

Player 10: . . . ran to the prize booth.

Player 11: When they looked at their tickets, they . . .

Player 12: . . . realized that they each had fifteen points. Their contest was a tie.

A variation of the continuing story is often a hit with older players. We have found that even university students enjoy the challenge of only adding one word at a time. The following example shows how one story begins. It continues this way until the story is complete.

RULE REMINDERS

- Ask players to sit in a circle.
- No repeated words are allowed.
- No think time sounds are allowed.
- Players who take too long to contribute are eliminated.
- Players who are eliminated should leave the circle.

Example:

Leader: Once

Player 1: upon

Player 2: a

Player 3: time

Player 4: there

Player 5: there (player is eliminated)

Player 6: was

Player 7: um (player is eliminated)

Player 8: a

Player 9: brave

Player 10: knight.

No matter how the activity is played, it can generate a lot of excitement when only a few players remain as contributors.

For those classmates who are watching, suspense is added as they wonder who will triumph. For all players, the exercise reinforces active listening.

Group Story Activity:
Good News/Bad News

"Good News/Bad News" provides players with the opportunity to see how reversals in a character's fortunes can change the direction of a plot. In this activity, plot is moved forward by complications in the action. Story structure (language arts) can be taught by alternating positive and negative events. Each player's contribution is thought of as an episode that moves the action forward.

Begin with the leader starting an original story. This first scene should end positively. The following player then continues the story, changing the situation negatively. The next player adds a positive scene, and that is followed by a negative one. The activity continues this way until the final player concludes the story.

Example: "Miguel's Money"

Leader: Miguel had been doing chores around the house and babysitting so that he could earn extra money. He really wanted to go on a class trip to the state capital, and his parents had given him permission to go, on one condition: Miguel had to pay for a portion of the trip himself. They would pay his travel costs, but he had to earn enough money for food and souvenirs. Miguel had worked for several months and had carefully put his money in a box atop his dresser. Every night before he went to sleep, he opened the box and counted his money. He needed one hundred dollars, and he almost had enough.

Player 1: On Saturday, Miguel helped his elderly neighbor by carrying groceries from her car into her house and helping her put them away. She tipped him two dollars. Miguel thanked her and ran home to put the money in the box. When he opened the box, however, he knew immediately that something was wrong. The money was gone!

Player 2: Miguel was frantic. He searched all around his room, including under the bed, in every dresser drawer, and in the closet. What could have happened to his savings? Miguel ran to the kitchen to tell his mother about the missing money. She smiled and told him not to worry. She assured him that everything would be all right.

Player 3: Miguel, however, was worried. The trip was in two weeks and he would never be able to earn enough money again in that short a time. He was angry and disappointed. His mother had not understood the seriousness of the situation. Worse, Miguel was certain that his father would accuse him of being irresponsible. He felt like all of his hard work had been for nothing. He sat on his bed and tried to hold back the tears welling in his eyes.

Player 4: Just then, Miguel's father appeared. He walked over to Miguel and sat next to him. "Son," he said, "I thought that you might like to have this." He held out a one hundred dollar bill. "I checked your money box. You had a lot of cash, and it almost totaled one hundred dollars. Because you were working so hard, I made up the difference and exchanged your savings for this. Enjoy your trip." Miguel felt so relieved. He hugged his father. He was grateful that the money was safe. More than that, he was pleased that his father had recognized his hard work.

This example is coherent and logical in its plot development. This, however, will not always be the case. The story may become more fantastic as more players contribute. The example below has more elaborate and less believable plot twists.

Example: "Davey and the Dog"

Leader: Davey only wanted one thing. He had his heart set on getting a puppy. He had begged his mother to let him have a pet. Every time he asked her for a puppy, she just said, "You can have one when you are a little older." One day, Davey was playing in his front yard when he heard a dog barking.

Player 1: "I'm going to find out where that dog is," thought Davey, and he started running toward the sound. He ran down the sidewalk, and before long he saw a small, sad puppy sitting in the street. He ran to the puppy and picked it up. As he did, a voice from behind him yelled, "Put my dog down, you little thief."

Player 2: "I didn't steal the dog," said Davey as he held out the puppy to a tall lady in a cape. "I just wanted to make sure he didn't get hurt." When he said this, the dog licked his face affectionately.

Player 3: The lady reached out and grabbed the dog. "I'll teach you a lesson," said the lady. "I am a space alien and I'm going to take this dog to my planet. You'll never see it again." With that, she twirled her cape, and she and the dog disappeared.

Player 4: Davey couldn't believe what had just happened. Where had they gone? Then he heard barking. The dog was nearby. He had to find him. "Puppy," he called, "where are you?" "Here," said the dog.

Player 5: Had the dog just spoken? Davey thought he must have imagined it. "Help me," called the puppy. "I can't find you," said Davey.

Player 6: A bird flew down from a tree branch and perched on Davey's shoulder. "Follow me," tweeted the bird, and she flew away. Davey ran fast, and he managed to keep the bird in sight.

Player 7: The bird led Davey to a strange looking rocket ship. He could see the lady opening the door, ready to head into space.

Player 8: Davey yelled, "Jump!" The puppy leapt out of the lady's arms and ran to him. Seeing this, the alien ran into the ship and blasted off. Davey and the dog watched as the space ship carried her into the clouds and out of sight.

Player 9: "I'm going to stay here with you," the puppy said to Davey. "You can't. My mother says I'm not old enough to have a dog. She won't let me keep a talking dog. That's certain."

Player 10: "I will only talk to you. She'll never know about my secret talent. Let's go home," said the small animal, and they walked to Davey's house. His mother was waiting on the front porch. "Davey," said his mother, "I've been thinking. Having a pet will teach you responsibility." She pointed to the dog. "This one looks like a stray. If he does not belong to anyone, you can keep him." Davey hugged his mother and the dog. "Arf," barked Davey's new pet happily.

Continuing stories and "Good News/ Bad News" are building blocks for story creation and improvisation, covered in the next chapter. They are foundations for more advanced types of stories.

REPRESENTATIVE SONGS
All Around the Kitchen
All Night, All Day
America

America, the Beautiful
Battle Hymn of the Republic
Bingo
Blue-Tail Fly
Charlie over the Ocean
Chim Chim Cher-ee
Clap Your Hands
Clementine
Colors of the Wind
Deedle Deedle Dumpling
Dixie
Do-Re-Mi
Eensy Weensy Spider
The Erie Canal
Ezekiel Saw the Wheel
Going over the Sea
He's Got the Whole World in His
    Hands
Home on the Range
Hush, Little Baby
If I Had a Hammer
If You're Happy
It's a Small World
It's Not Easy Being Green
I've Been Working on the Railroad
Jingle Bells
Kookaburra
Little Sally Water
Long-Legged Sailor
Marching to Pretoria
Michael, Row the Boat Ashore
Mighty Pretty Motion
O, Susanna
Old Dan Tucker
Old Joe Clark
Old MacDonald
Over the River and through the Wood
Polly Wolly Doodle
Rain, Rain, Go Away
Sally Go Round the Sun
Scotland's Burning
See Saw, Margery Daw
She'll Be Comin' Round the Mountain
Shoo, Fly
Sing
Skip to My Lou
The Star-Spangled Banner
This Land Is Your Land

This Old Man
Under the Sea
When the Saints Go Marching In
Who's That Yonder
Wind up the Apple Tree
With a Little Help from My Friends
Yankee Doodle
You're a Grand Old Flag

SAMPLE LESSON, CHAPTER 5

LESSON OVERVIEW: This lesson integrates creative drama and music activities with social studies and language arts. Using a journeys theme, the lesson invites students to learn about personal, emotional, and physical journeys as well as about cultures.

RECOMMENDED GRADE: 6

CONTENT AREAS: drama/theatre, music, social studies, and language arts

INSTRUCTIONAL OBJECTIVES:

- Players will compare various types of journeys. (Social studies)
- Players will establish context, plot, and point of view in narrative presentations. (Language arts)
- Players will create characters, environments, and actions based upon personal experience, heritage, history, and imagination. (Drama/theatre)
- Players will sing accurately and with expression. (Music)

LENGTH OF LESSON: thirty to forty-five minutes

MATERIALS:

recording of "Wreck of the *Edmund
    Fitzgerald*"
(lyrics can be found at gordonlightfoot.
    com/WreckoftheEdmundFitzgerald
    .shtml)
American Gothic by Grant Wood
Image can be found at www.artic.edu/
    artaccess/AA_Modern/pages/
    MOD_5.shtml)

ACTIVITIES AND PROCEDURES:

Vocal Expression: Word Painting with the Voice

In this activity, players have an opportunity to express themselves through writing their names and "painting" them vocally. If computers are available, players may use software fonts to illustrate their names in different ways. Otherwise, players will need to write or draw their names in at least three different styles, using a variety of paper, colors, and type faces—such as in big, bold, black capital letters; in small, swirly, pink italics; and in ball-point pen using normal handwriting. They should do the same for places that they would like to visit or explore. From these styles, they are to find different ways of expressing their names and these places through their voices.

Characterization Activity: American Gothic

Using Grant Wood's famous painting, *American Gothic*, ask players to create an autobiography for either of the characters. Stipulate that the story must include information about how the character came to live on the farm seen in the background. Speaking in first person, each player shares the character's life story.

Group Story Activity: Good News/Bad News

The following paragraph is the beginning of the story "Mei Meets Her New Family." It is an original story of a personal journey, in which positive and negative episodes are alternated. After completing the story, invite students to decide where Mei is journeying from and to report upon the culture of that country.

"Mei Meets Her New Family"
Mei wasn't sure what to expect when she stepped from the plane. She didn't remember her birth parents, and she was excited that she had been adopted. She also was pleased and a little scared that her home now would be in America. She knew that Mr. and Mrs. Glass would be waiting for her inside the terminal, and she promised herself that she would be a good daughter and make them proud of her.

Ensemble Singing: "This Land Is Your Land"

The two previous creative drama activities have had the United States as their setting. This is a good time to introduce a well-known song about this country.

Woody Guthrie wrote the words and music to the song "This Land Is Your Land." Many recordings are available for players to hear, and the lyrics are available online. Once players know the tune and lyrics and the leader has provided the pitch, engage in ensemble singing. As a replay, leaders and players with more advanced musical backgrounds might want to create and sing harmonies.

After singing, ask players to locate on a map the areas of the country referenced in the song. Which states, for example, are known for their wheat fields? Next, invite them to trace routes taken by settlers as they moved from east to west, or to identify migration patterns from one geographic region to another. Ask them to consider what prompted these migrations.

Group Story Activity: The Continuing Story

"Ian's Journey to Space" is played with participants either sitting or standing in a circle. When the leader points to someone, that player continues the story. Those who repeat words or otherwise err take their seats. The game concludes when only one player remains.

"Ian's Journey to Space"
Ian strapped himself into the cockpit. It was a dangerous mission, but he felt prepared. He knew that someone had to fly to the space station because ground control had been receiving troubling signals from deep space for days. He looked over his shoulder as the seat began to rumble from the force of leaving the earth.
(The leader now calls on others to continue.)

After completing the story, ask students to research missions that American astronauts have taken. Compare these to Ian's mission.

Ensemble Activity: "The Wreck of the Edmund Fitzgerald"
The leader discusses different types of missions, such as *Mission: Impossible*, space missions, "mission accomplished," and mission failure. The leader distinguishes between true and fictional stories, introducing the crew of the Edmond Fitzgerald to illustrate an important mission that failed. After the players research the legend of the wreck of the ship (reviewing the Great Lakes and solving the mystery of which is Gitche Gumee), they listen to the song as performed by Gordon Lightfoot (available on line). Players trace the drama as events unfold and identify words or phrases that are appropriate for expressive enhancement (such as word painting, body sound accompaniment, found sound effects, etc.). The players practice select sounds that will accompany the song, with attention to providing dramatic support for the story line.

ASSESSMENT: Complete the rubric shown in table 5.7.

Table 5.7. Rubric for Sample Lesson

	Yes	No	In part
Players can identify physical, emotional, and personal journeys in the activities and can articulate the differences and similarities among them.			
Players can incorporate context, plot, and point of view into original stories.			
Players can incorporate characters, settings, and dramatic action into original stories.			
Players use vocal expression in speaking and singing.			

CHAPTER 6

Improvisation and Story Creation

Having building blocks in place, the leader and players are now ready for some of the more difficult, challenging, and rewarding activities in both art forms. Greater spontaneity is introduced in the forms of open-ended stories, improvisations, and **role playing**. These activities are more demanding. Players will creatively explore their possibilities within more open structures.

STORY CREATION
(LOWER/UPPER LEVELS)

Players may wish to create stories as a way to exercise their imaginations. With these activities, creative drama sessions become more student directed. Players come together cooperatively to share ideas, plan, dramatize, and evaluate. Story creation stresses artistic, social, and communication skills. In addition, it may generate material for story dramatization.

Activities can be conducted in several ways. Some activities are brief, while others require more time and include developing and dramatizing complicated stories. With oral and written options, story creation activities relate directly to the language arts curriculum. The leader's choices here should depend upon session learning goals.

Brainstorming is a helpful process to employ during story creation activities. This technique involves thinking of as many ideas as possible. These are recorded. After a number of ideas have been offered, each is considered for its merits and dramatic potential. The best ideas can then be tried.

Creating stories gives players practice with elements such as plot development, characterization, and dialogue creation. The activities that follow illustrate the close connection that creative drama can have with language arts.

Story Creation Activity:
What Happens Next?
Working in groups, players use a familiar nursery rhyme, poem, song, or story as the story core. Each group then determines "what happens next" and dramatizes its story. There are limitless possibilities for developing complications and giving new direction to familiar material.

Example 1:
Jack and Jill went up the hill
To fetch a pail of water;
Jack fell down and broke his crown,
And Jill came tumbling after.

The players might create a dramatization in which passing villagers find the unlucky pair. They summon the local physician, who administers first aid to Jill and takes Jack to the hospital.

Example 2:
> Humpty Dumpty sat on a wall,
> Humpty Dumpty had a great fall.
> All the king's horses,
> And all the king's men,
> Couldn't put Humpty together again.

The players might create a dramatization that shows the men trying and failing to put Humpty together. They leave the scene. Then one player returns with some glue and repairs Humpty, who returns happily to his place on the wall.

Story Creation Activity:
First Line of a Story
Players are given only an opening line. They work in groups, and each is responsible for developing, casting, and dramatizing a complete story.

Using the opening lines below, players should work together to develop the plot, create and cast characters, rehearse, and perform. When groups work with the same opening line, evaluation can focus upon differences and similarities in their stories. Replay may be desirable.

Writing can extend the activity, with players making new stories or recording those they have created.

Examples:
> The old house creaked and moaned as
> the storm grew fiercer.
> Mara and Shirley were alone in the
> cabin.
> Robert had never been this nervous.
> The old man took a deep breath and
> rang the doorbell.

STORY CREATION FROM PROPS (UPPER LEVEL)

Stories can evolve from props. These are versatile, have concrete form, can be used as intended or differently, and appeal to the imagination. They can serve as the basis for simple tales shared orally, become the inspiration for more complicated work, or suggest and embellish a characterization. Players may incorporate one or more props into a story.

Story Creation from Props Activity:
Oral Story Creation
With everyone seated in a circle, the leader introduces a prop. Players are invited to think of a story in which the prop is mentioned. When they are ready to share their ideas, players should raise their hands. Each player is responsible for a complete story. The most interesting ones can be dramatized.

Example:

Leader: Today's prop is an umbrella. Think of a story that has an umbrella in it. I'll pass this around so that everyone can look at it, then we'll hear some of your ideas.

Player 1: As I was getting ready to go to school the other day, my dad said, "Don't forget to take your umbrella with you." The sun was shining so brightly I couldn't believe it was going to rain. I felt really foolish walking to school carrying an umbrella. But by the end of the day, the sky had turned dark. As I was walking home, it began to pour. I opened my umbrella and smiled as I walked through the raindrops.

Player 2: My mom told me to clean out my closet. She gave me a big box and told me to put things I no longer wanted into it. I started on the top shelf where I kept my hats, scarves, and gloves. I put a few pairs of gloves that were now too small for me in the box. I did the same thing with two hats that I had not worn in several years. Then I folded my scarves. I would not need them until next winter, but I wanted to keep them. Then I reached to the very back of the closet and felt something odd. This was not something to wear. I pulled out the object and, to my surprise, saw that it was an umbrella that I thought I had lost. I was not putting this in the box. I was keeping my umbrella and would use it the next time it rained.

Story Creation from Props Activity: What Is It?

Old items stored in an attic or basement, unusual gadgets, and other miscellaneous items are all suitable for this activity. In fact, the only requirements are that the prop cannot be easily identified by the players and cannot be dangerous. The leader shows the prop and asks the players to create a story about it or how it might be used. The purpose of this exercise is to stimulate imagination; correct identification of the object is not necessary.

Example:

> Leader: (Holds up a hairbrush with a missing handle.) Let's use our imaginations and share our ideas. What do you think this item is, and how might it be used?
>
> Player 1: I think it is a new kind of paintbrush. You dip it in the paint and then swirl it on what you're painting. It's a quick and easy way to make designs.
>
> Leader: Please tell us a story involving the paintbrush.

Story Creation from Props Activity: Who Used It?

In this format, the prop used may or may not be one that is easily recognized. Costume pieces and hats also work well here. The leader asks for the object's real or invented name and a description of its use, and asks players to decide who might

STORY CREATION FROM PROPS

- appropriate for older players
- can be played individually, in pairs, or in groups

have used it. Answers must be incorporated into a story. As before, the emphasis should be on imaginative response rather than accurate identification.

Example:

> Leader: (Holds up a colander.) What might this be? How does it work? Who used it?
>
> Player 1: The object is called a *steamerator* and is a part of a shower. It works like a showerhead, and people use it when bathing. In my story, an old man uses the steamerator.
>
> Once there was an old man who lived by himself in the forest. He had lived in a nice house once, but he didn't like it and moved into the woods. The only thing he missed having in the woods was a shower. One day the old man had an idea. He rummaged through a box containing things from his old house and pulled out the steamerator and some rope. He strung the rope through the handles and then tied his unusual shower head to a tall tree branch. He waited. Soon it began to rain. The old man stood under his newly constructed shower and bathed in the rain as it fell through the holes.

Story Creation from Props Activity: Finding a New Use

Players are shown an easily recognized prop. They are asked to identify it and to show how it is normally used. Next, they are asked to invent and demonstrate a new use for it. This can be followed by creating and dramatizing commercials for the item's new function.

Example:

A player is shown a bowl. After correctly identifying it and pantomiming mixing something in it, she puts it on her head and says that it is the latest fashion in hats. She next creates and presents a commercial for the hat.

Story Creation from Props Activity: Prop Grab Bags

Before beginning this activity, the leader should prepare bags containing at least three props each. Items should be unrelated. Players form groups, and each group is given a grab bag. Time is allowed for examining the props. A story incorporating them is developed and rehearsed. The props may be used either realistically or in ways that better suit the story. The spoon in bag 1 below, for example, might become a shovel for a pixie.

These are examples of grab bag contents.

Examples:

Bag 1: spoon, ball, mitten
Bag 2: seashell, feather, cell phone
Bag 3: bell, drinking straw, candle
Bag 4: apple, towel, notebook
Bag 5: eraser, vase, necklace

STORY CREATION FROM PICTURES (UPPER LEVEL)

As a resource, the leader will want to maintain a file containing prints, photographs, and pictures. These should be laminated or in some other way preserved so that they are not damaged or destroyed by use. Depictions of people work best, with subjects ranging from individuals to large gatherings. Be sure to include various age and ethnic groups.

Story Creation from Pictures Activity: Every Picture Tells a Story

This can be a simple oral activity or the basis of a dramatization. Options for leading the activity begin with showing a picture and include (1) having individuals contribute story ideas; (2) grouping the players and having each plan, rehearse, and play a story; and (3) giving each group a different picture. Depending on group size, adding characters or double casting may be necessary.

Example:

The picture is of a large group of people gathering at a picnic. Several are clustered around a telephone talking to someone. The players create a story about a family reunion. Their characters include a grandmother, grandfather, husband, wife, aunt, and small child. The action centers on a telephone conversation with another person who is unable to attend.

OPEN-ENDED STORIES (LOWER/UPPER LEVELS)

Open-ended stories are incomplete stories that can be developed orally, in writing, or through dramatization. They provide practice in language arts areas such as speaking, listening, and writing. Players must carefully pay attention, adapt, and respond.

In this activity, the leader provides the beginning of a story and then calls on players to continue. Normally, three to five players carry the story forward, with the final person's addition being the conclusion. Limiting the number of players who add helps keep the story from becoming confusing. To include more participants, replay by repeating the opening and calling on new players. The only stipulation is that the plot must go in a new direction. Each version must be different from previous ones.

Take care when preparing beginnings to keep them open-ended. A common error occurs when the leader has a plot in mind. Remember that there is no limit to the stories that can come from a truly open-ended starter. Stories can be stopped anywhere, even in the middle of a sentence.

When players are first introduced to this activity, they may add only a few words or a sentence. A goal should be to have them contribute as much as possible. The more twists and turns a plot takes, the more creative and interesting the results. Capturing the completed stories provides a resource for later story dramatizations.

Open-Ended Story

The following samples illustrate how stories can develop differently from a shared beginning. Both versions use the same starter. The versions show how the stories can go in different directions.

> Leader: There once was a brave king named Freddie the Fantastic. He ruled the Kingdom of Mononga and kept the people there safe from the evil ogre who lived atop a hill just outside of the kingdom. One day, the ogre decided that it would be fun to frighten the king's subjects. So . . .

Version 1:

> Player 1: . . . he left his hilltop home and walked to Mononga. As soon as the people saw him, they began to scream and run into their homes.

> Player 2: When Freddie the Fantastic heard his subjects, he decided to see what was wrong. He walked outside of his palace and came face to face with the ogre.

> Player 3: "Ah, ha!" said the ogre. "It will be great fun to frighten a king. You will now see how scary I can be."

> Player 4: "I'm not afraid of you," said Freddie. "Show me your scariest trick. If I am not frightened, you must agree to leave this kingdom in peace forever."

> Player 5: "I agree," said the ogre. "Watch this." With that, he turned himself into a fire breathing dragon.

> Player 6: King Freddie was undaunted. He reached for a bucket of water that he kept by the palace door. He threw the water and extinguished the dragon's fire.

> Player 7: "You won," said the ogre. He retreated to his hilltop home and was never seen in Mononga again.

Version 2:

> Player 1: . . . he started walking toward the kingdom. Before long, he came to a meadow where he saw a lovely girl picking flowers. He stopped.

> Player 2: The girl looked up and smiled at him. "Hello," she said. "I am Princess Frieda the Feisty. Who are you?"

> Player 3: The ogre was speechless. He had never seen such a pretty girl. At last he said, "Aren't you afraid of me?"

> Player 4: "Why, no. Why should I be?" asked Frieda. She held out her hand and the ogre shook it.

> Player 5: Just then Freddie the Fantastic approached on his horse. "Don't touch my daughter," he commanded. "Frieda," he called. "I will protect you just as I protect my subjects from this nasty ogre." He drew his sword and prepared to attack the ogre.

> Player 6: "Father, stop that," said Frieda. "He is a kind ogre. You have

misunderstood him." She approached the ogre. "I am pleased to meet you," she said, and she shook his hand.

Player 7: The ogre smiled. "I did not know that there were kind people like you in Mononga," he said. "I will never frighten you or the people in your kingdom again. We are friends now."

Open-Ended Story, Variation 1

In this variation, it is the players who call on others to add to the story. The leader only calls on the first player.

"The Day of the Game"
Jeff was so nervous that he could hardly eat supper. All summer his Little League team had worked hard, and they had made it to the play-offs. Tonight was the big game! Dad had promised he would take Jeff to the field and then stay and watch the game, but it was nearly time to leave and Dad wasn't home from work yet. As Jeff sat at the dinner table and picked at his food, his mother said, "I'm not going to allow you to play if you don't eat your dinner." "She doesn't understand," Jeff muttered to himself. Just then the phone rang. Jeff . . .

Open-Ended Story, Variation 2

Another option is to provide the story starter orally or in writing, and then give the players time to write the rest of the story. Players can work individually or in small groups, and their stories can then be read aloud, adding writing, reading, and speaking to the language arts skills addressed. Any of the open-ended story examples in this text can be used this way. "Wheels" is provided below for practice.

"Wheels"
Julio longed to have a new bike, but he was too young to get a job and he hadn't saved enough allowance money to buy even a used ten-speed. Every day, as he walked home from school, he stopped in front of Wesley's Wheels, the local bike shop, and looked at all of the shiny new models in the window. One day, as he stood in front of the shop window, a man came out of the store. He . . .

Open-Ended Story, Variation 3

The leader shares the opening of the story with the group, repeating it at least twice so that players grasp essential information. They then form small groups to devise and dramatize an ending. This strategy requires that players plan together, develop quick thinking skills, and respect each other's ideas. The leader should check with each group during planning to see if their ideas are dramatically feasible. Rehearsal time is helpful, to eliminate rough spots and build confidence before stories are enacted.

The number of players in a group will, in some way, influence the direction of the story. If the leader's opening has only four characters, but there are five in the group, the players might create another character. Should a group of four players decide that their story needs five characters, some doubling will be necessary. In other words, one person would play two parts. The following story mentions only one person and can be practiced for incorporating more characters.

"March Morning"
It was a cold, windy March morning and, as on every other morning, I was to meet the school bus at the end of the lane in ten minutes. I started walking, and a few snowflakes fell to the ground. With each step, more and more snow fell, but I forced myself to continue, finding it harder and harder to see. With the wind coming into my face, it seemed as though I could not take

another step. I could not move one more inch when . . .

IMPROVISATION AND MUSIC (LOWER/UPPER LEVELS)

Improvisation is one of America's indigenous musical idioms that players can enjoy at an early age. Older players often surprise themselves with the stunning musical outcomes of improvisational activities. One of the keys to success in facilitating improvisational activities is to help young players develop a vocabulary of melodic and rhythmic patterns that can be incorporated into the free invention of "new" material. Many of the activities in chapters 2, 3, 4, and 5 have built a vocabulary of rhythmic patterns and sound sources. The wider the vocabulary players have, the more freedom and choices they have in their creative work. Improvisation involves the spontaneous reordering and re-creating of ideas. Players, however, must have some ideas for starters.

Vocal and instrumental improvisation is especially enjoyable. However, many children are self-conscious about singing, so the leader might begin improvisation with instrumental exploration, a more comfortable starting point—particularly for older players. The speaking and singing voices are wonderful, personal instruments that will be incorporated after the concept of improvisation is secure and players are more confident with it.

In the following activities, traditional instruments (e.g., piano, electronic keyboard, xylophone, resonator bells) are often suggested. Homemade options, however, often provide more interesting and challenging potentials in the creative process. Tuned glasses or bottles filled with liquid, for instance, serve as appropriate sound sources for improvisation if more traditional instruments are not available. Be certain to fill glasses or bottles with varying levels of liquid to provide different pitch levels.

SOLO ACTIVITIES

Solo Improvisation Activity: Introduction to Pitch Level
For this activity, players will need different tones (such as three resonator bells) and one mallet. Three tones of the keyboard also will work. Given four minutes, they are to improvise a thirty-second composition using the three tones. Within their explorations, their learning task is to demonstrate melodic direction—all of the different ways the tones can be sequenced. Players should determine the highest and lowest tones and invent patterns that change melodic direction.

A second learning point from this activity is awareness of music's form. All improvisations require form, or they will sound aimless and incoherent. The player's piece should involve some repetition of the same pitch or pattern, and it should involve some **contrast**. The leader's guidance will be needed to help players use both repetition and contrast. The leader may encourage the players, for instance, to change the duration (length) of the tones and experiment with the tempo (speed) of the composition. As players listen to one another's improvisations, they should compare and contrast the directions in which the melodies move. They may also comment on the form of the piece.

Solo Improvisation Activity: A Season for Two Hands
Players will use two mallets and four or five distinct pitches in this activity. Pitched bottles work well. For different tone colors, the leader may demonstrate a variety of objects to use as mallets, such as wooden pencils, spoons, rulers, keys,

metal pens or mechanical pencils, and so on. The task is for the players to improvise a forty-five-second piece describing one of the seasons.

After listening to one another's improvisations, the players identify which season is being portrayed. The chosen season should not be revealed until the discussion concludes. The leader steers discussion towards elements of music (rhythm, melody, dynamics, tempo, tone color, style) that might support season titles. Students can then discuss elements of weather as a curricular connection.

Solo Improvisation Activity:
Improvising for Movement
This exercise involves using two mallets with bells, bottles, or both hands on the black keys of the piano. Players improvise a one-minute composition for dance. As players imagine the improvisation, they have the opportunity to decide what type of dancing will be appropriate and mentally plan the "choreography." Encourage them to listen for the melodic direction (moving upward or downward) and rhythmic movement (tempo, duration) to give clues to the dancer.

There is a time lag between what is heard and when the movement is executed, so ask one player to musically perform the improvisation while the rest of the players plan the movement. As the musical improvisation is repeated, the dancers are more prepared to improvise movements appropriately. When players improvise, they rely completely on the music to inspire movements. There are no verbal directions.

Solo Improvisation Activity:
Improvising Background Music
for Advertisements
For this game, players will need a number of pictures advertising products or services.

Cruise ship brochures showing a calm sea; mountain bike ads; ads for diamond watches; ads that depict healthful eating; and those showing narrow streets with crowds of people in foreign cities are good examples of strikingly different advertisements. After looking at these, players can be inspired to improvise supporting music.

Players should select an ad and determine how many tones are needed to improvise suitable music. Their improvisation should be designed, for example, to persuade the audience to visit the country, buy the product, or agree with the idea being advertised.

The improvisation may last only one minute. During the preparation, players must examine the visual material closely.

QUESTIONS RELATED TO ELEMENTS OF MUSIC

- Are colors used? How bright or dull are they?
- Describe any patterns.
- Where is there repetition or contrast?
- Are bold letters or soft lines involved? If so, where?
- What mood is created?

Solo Improvisation Activity:
Advertising the Future
This improvisation exercise is for advanced players working in teams of two. The session begins by imagining what the world will be like fifty years from now. What will everyday life consist of—work, school, sports, leisure, and so on? Players determine products or services that might be needed in the future, for example, homework machines that automatically do all assignments or individual

flight planners that chart our astro-travel. Each team dreams up one product or service that they would like to advertise.

The goal of this game is to prepare ad copy (text) and/or lyrics to go along with the music. With the futuristic product/service in mind, ask players to improvise suitable rhythms and melodies for a jingle that will appear on video. Some teams may wish to prepare props or other visuals to demonstrate the product or service. Should they cast and play their commercial, they bridge to characterization in creative drama. As a general rule, the players' preparation takes far more time than the resulting two-minute performance.

ENSEMBLE ACTIVITIES

Ensemble Improvisation Activity: Dynamic Domino Effect

The leader begins with a simple three- to four-note melodic pattern (such as G, C, A, G) and invites each player to echo it on an instrument. At a moderate volume, the first player performs the pattern. Each subsequent player may adjust the volume by playing the echo one degree louder or softer. The "wave" of repetition can grow gradually softer or louder; however, it must grow by degrees.

At the point when the pattern is almost inaudible or very loud, the next player improvises a new pattern. A new "Domino Effect" is then established.

Rhythmic Dialogue Activity: Nursery Rhyme

For this, players will need instruments such as resonator bells or xylophones. The leader rehearses the lyrics and rhythm to "Baa, Baa, Black Sheep." Then the leader divides players into teams of two for sharing an improvised dialogue. One of the players uses the rhythm to improvise new pitches for the question, "Baa, baa, black sheep, have you any wool?" The other player will perform a rhythmic response with a new melodic improvisation to the rhythm, "Yes, sir, yes, sir, three bags full. One for my master, one for my dame, and one for the little boy who lives down the lane." After the players reverse roles, they may be invited to try out different improvisations.

Ensemble Improvisation Activity: Instant Opera

Ensemble activities are dependent upon players carefully listening and musically responding to one another. That is when improvisation becomes more meaningful and sensitive. Sometimes, for example, a rhythmic or tonal pattern is imitated and manipulated back and forth throughout the entire group. It serves as the kernel and grows to a full, well-developed improvisation. In the ensemble improvisations that follow, players might be encouraged to think of their role in the group as both active performer and active listener.

"Instant Opera" can be played for a few moments or expanded into a thirty-minute lesson. It involves improvising a scenario or brief operetta in a short period of time. For young players, the leader might select three tones, such as E, G, and A. The leader vocalizes all conversation on the E, G, or A tones. Everyone sings questions and responses. Through discussion and critique, the best way to sing questions or statements of surprise, sadness, and so on will emerge. Demonstrations will help confirm good operatic musical choices. Players should experiment by confining communication to one single tone (as a monotone) and discovering what results from such limitations before adding additional tones for effect.

Depending on the age level of the players, nursery rhymes, poems, or stories can be expanded into opera by singing the unfolding of events. Segments can be improvised using vocal sounds as well. Players delight in imitating video games, animals, machines, appliances, and other sound effects.

Ensemble Improvisation Activity: Name Game, Expanded

Improvisations can be built upon familiar activities such as the "Name Game" in chapter 2. Here, players improvise an ensemble composition by using everyone's name. The following steps will prepare a good outcome: (1) chanting everyone's name; (2) rhythmically clapping each name together as a group; (3) inviting each player to improvise his or her name on instruments using melodic tones; and (4) performing each player's name on instruments as a complete ensemble.

Leaders can keep the improvisation together by accompanying it with a two-tone chord (e.g., C and G) on the beat. What follows is a suggested introduction that establishes the beat and tempo for a solid start:

> Names, names, names are fine.
> You say yours; I'll say mine.
> Put them all in a line.

The improvisation closes with a slight revision to the rhyme:

> Names, names, names are fine.
> You said yours; I said mine.
> Put them all in a line.
> That's the end of our rhyme.

Ensemble Improvisation Activity: Name Game, Variation 1

Advanced players may create more texture for the performance, which requires careful concentration. First, all players practice the performance. Then the order of the names is reversed and practiced as "backward." Dividing the ensemble into two groups, experiment with half of the group performing the chant forward while half perform it backward. To be successful, players should not be distracted by the other group's contrasting sounds.

Ensemble Improvisation Activity: Name Game, Variation 2

This game involves an add-a-name dimension in the improvisation and is a challenge for advanced players. One player performs his or her name continuously while each additional person enters with his or her name. By the time the last one enters, the improvisation has become thicker, louder, and busier.

IMPROVISATIONS IN CREATIVE DRAMA

As in music, creative drama **improvisations** require spontaneity, careful listening, and concentration. Improvisations challenge players to work within the boundaries of a scenario structured upon given information. These can be very open or more prescribed, but either way they result in a variety of interpretations.

Givens in creative drama can include the following:

- Who: characters
- What: conflict or problem
- When: time
- Where: setting or place of action
- How: interpretation

An improvisation can be based upon all five givens or as few as two. Of the five, *who* and *what* are essential; *how* is most often omitted.

In its purest form, performance proceeds without planning time. Givens are announced, and the playing begins. Action and dialogue are contributed as the story evolves, precluding players from mapping out the direction the plot will take. In creative drama, however, the total absence of planning tends to be inhibiting, particularly to novices. A minute or so, therefore, should be allowed for players to determine casting, setting, and whether or not to use dialogue. Any discussion of plot, including specific actions and dialogue, should be avoided.

The following approach is recommended:

1. Select players for the cast.
2. Give the cast the scenario (two to five givens).
3. Allow them to decide who will play each role, whether they will use pantomime or dialogue, and what setting, if any, is needed.
4. Begin play.

The more information is known to the players, the more structured an improvisation becomes. The leader's purpose will determine how much information is provided. If seeing how well the cast can create their own characterizations is important, the leader should give minimal descriptions, as in improvisation 1 below. If, however, a goal is to see how precisely a character can be portrayed, the leader should give a more complete description, as in improvisation 2.

Improvisation 1:
Who: A boy and a girl.
What: Studying for a test. Neither is interested in the subject, and they must keep each other motivated.
Where: The library.
When: The evening before the test.
How: Casually.

Improvisation 2:
Who: A boy and a girl. He is flunking the course and wants her help. She is a straight A student.
What: Studying for a test. He must pass the exam. She does not want to help him.
Where: The library.
When: The evening before the test.
How: He is nervous; she is confident.

Improvisations can be changed merely by altering one of the givens, as in these next examples. Here, players see the influence of setting on character relationships. It is unlikely that a student and teacher would relate to each other in the same way in a professional situation (office) as they would in a social one (party).

Improvisation 3:
Who: A teacher and a student.
What: The student wants the teacher to change a grade. The teacher does not believe grades should be changed.
Where: The teacher's office.

Improvisation 4:
Who: A teacher and a student.
What: The student wants the teacher to change a grade. The teacher does not believe grades should be changed.
Where: At a party.

During an improvisation, players do not know what will happen; therefore, they cannot predetermine the action. They must listen and watch carefully and respond to their partners, adapting to action. When they respond to the immediate action, they are **playing the moment**. Not doing so moves the improvisation off course.

- players request more planning time;
- players need assistance with the format;
- experiences tend to be short and funny;
- players get stuck.

There are occasions when players might be skilled enough to spontaneously create action but not words. These players may only be ready to improvise using pantomime. If this is the case, improvisations with dialogue can be introduced later. Whenever it is used, dialogue should suit the character, situation, dramatic action, and type of story.

Improvisations may be humorous or serious. The direction often depends on the leader's guidance, and the leader's positive reinforcement of players who create an appropriate tone for their scene. Successful improvisation requires patience and getting comfortable with the activity's framework.

The ideal way to end play is when the conflict is resolved and the action comes to a natural conclusion. When this does not occur, players may giggle or look helpless. Should this occur, the leader can enter into the playing **in role**. As a character asking questions, it may be possible for the leader to get the players back on track. Another choice, if the players get silly, is simply to stop the action.

IMPROVISATION AS STORY CREATION (LOWER/UPPER LEVELS)

Improvisations are closely related to stories. Some leaders use reading assignments for improvisation, so that young learners develop empathy for the characters, develop interest in literature, or engage in predicting what happens next. Improvisations can, in fact, be a form of story creation. An idea generated this way may be made into a story through replay or additional improvisation. The process lends itself to clarifying action, creating scenes, better understanding character interactions, and exploring story structure.

When players are having difficulty understanding relationships, they can improvise character interactions that may or may not be found in the story and then, with their new understanding, return to the original material. Likewise, they can improvise the scene before or after the story event. In these ways, improvisations have provided the seeds from which better comprehension could grow.

The examples that follow can be improvised to form the basis of a story.

Improvisation 1:
Who: Two children and a neighbor.
What: The neighbor catches the children using her lawn as a shortcut home from school. They do not have permission to be in her yard.
Where: The neighbor's front yard.
When: After school.

Improvisation 2:
Who: Two friends.
What: The friends find a wallet with money in it and must decide what to do with it.
Where: The playground.
When: Recess.

Improvisation 3:
Who: Two friends.
What: The friends find a wallet with money in it and must decide what to do with it. One wants to keep

it, and the other wants to turn it in to the school office.

Where: The school library.
When: After lunch.

Improvisations 2 and 3 are similar. Notice how changing the place and giving more information about the characters alters the playing of the scene.

Improvisation 4:
Who: A student and a neighbor.
What: The student is selling candy bars for a school club fundraiser. The neighbor is frugal.
Where: At the neighbor's front door.

ROLE PLAYING (UPPER LEVEL)

Role playing uses improvisation for exploring problems and issues. It is most useful when players act out situations that involve controversy or multiple options. Players may use this technique to

- test perceptions;
- propose solutions;
- debate alternative choices;
- examine various points of view;
- rationalize behaviors;
- participate in decision-making.

Scenarios are based on givens, with characters and conflicts clearly defined. During the course of the dramatization and in the crucial evaluation period following, players propose solutions, reveal motivating behaviors, articulate feelings, develop arguments, and try to understand the conflicting perspectives inherent in scenes.

A recommended pattern for role-playing is (1) play, (2) evaluate, (3) replay, with original cast members switching roles. This procedure allows players to view the conflict from more than one character's perspective. Discussion should address how the players felt in diverse roles and

what insights were gained in each. This activity provides older players with an opportunity to safely test reactions, broaden understanding, and demonstrate sensitivity to others.

Because this activity often deals with controversial or difficult situations, the possibility exists for strong emotions. Students could offer socially unacceptable or psychologically troubling responses. This risk should not deter the leader from using this challenging material. It should, however, underscore the need for calm and reasoned responses should intervention be necessary. Overreacting, giving undue attention to students, or arguing with them if they engage in this behavior is not recommended. If emotions are alarmingly raw or volatile, seek assistance from trained personnel.

Like improvisations in general, role-playing scenarios can be used repeatedly. The leader should not expect players to find the "right" answer; often there isn't one. The importance of role playing is that it opens discussion to the scope and substance of a problem.

Role Playing: "The Vandal"
Who: Maria (a student) and the principal.
What: Maria has seen a popular student commit an act of vandalism at school. If she tells what she knows, she fears other students will label her a snitch. She knows, however, that vandalism is wrong and should be reported. The principal has heard that Maria can identify the vandal and wants her to do so.
Where: The principal's office.

Questions:
- How will other students feel about Maria if she tells? If she doesn't tell?

How much should their opinions matter?
- How will Maria feel if she tells? If she doesn't tell?
- Do you think it is more important to be truthful or to be popular in this situation? Why?
- Under what circumstances, if any, is it acceptable to lie?

Role Playing: "The Curfew"

Who: Susan, her mother, and her stepfather.
When: After dinner.
What: Susan wants to stay out past her curfew, but her mother's new husband forbids it, and her mother agrees with him. Susan feels angry and neglected now that the family structure has changed. Her mother and stepfather feel that Susan is rebellious and unwilling to accept their authority.
Where: The family room.

Questions:
- What are some of the ways to handle disagreements between parents and children?
- What emotions might each of these characters realistically express during an argument about the curfew?

Role Playing: "The Test"

Who: Perry and Janice.
When: Before Perry's math class.
What: Perry is the team's best player, but he is failing math. He must pass his math exam if he is to remain eligible for sports. Without Perry, the team might lose the state championship. Janice, his girlfriend, has already taken the test, wants to help him, and offers to give Perry the answers. Perry knows it is wrong to cheat but he wants to play football.

Where: School.

Questions:
- The victories that Perry helps the team win generate a lot of school pride. In this way, he helps the whole school when he plays. Does this justify cheating? Why or why not?
- How do you feel about sports? Are they more important than academics?
- Support your opinions. Why do you feel this way?

Role-playing scenarios can lead to thought-provoking scenes. The questions used in conjunction with these scenarios are designed to produce a variety of responses.

SAMPLE LESSON, CHAPTER 6
LESSON OVERVIEW: This lesson integrates creative drama and music activities with language arts. Players will learn about story elements such as characters, plot structure, and foreshadowing by using voice, found sound, story creation, and improvisation skills.
RECOMMENDED GRADE: 4
CONTENT AREAS: drama/theatre, music, and language arts
INTRUCTIONAL OBJECTIVES:

- Players use language for learning, enjoyment, and the exchange of information. (Language arts)
- Players collaborate to select interrelated characters, environments, and situations for classroom dramatizations. (Drama/theatre)
- Players create and arrange music for readings or for dramatizations. (Music)

LENGTH OF LESSON: forty-five to sixty minutes
ACTIVITIES AND PROCEDURES:
Preparation: Review the definitions of *plot*, *characters*, and *setting* with the

players. Engage them in a discussion of what makes an interesting story.

Story Creation: "School of Fish"
Before playing, listen carefully to the section on fish in *Carnival of Animals*, first introduced in chapter 4. After listening, players should form groups. Invite each group to create a story inspired by the music. The title of the story is "School of Fish." Players should be given time to create and rehearse the story. Some groups may be quite literal in their interpretations and base their stories on what a group of fish does all day. Others may be more inspired and create a story about a school where the teacher and the students are fish. There are many options, and the players will enjoy performing their stories for classmates.

Improvising Tone Colors: Fish Timbre
After performing "School of Fish" stories, players research different types of fish, from guppies to sharks. Focusing on the different characteristics of the fish (e.g., size, weight, speed, activity in water), players find an appropriate sound to portray one fish for performance with the *Carnival of Animals* music. In small groups, add the sounds to the recording, and discuss the match between the sounds and the fish characteristics.

Open-Ended Story: "Winter Fun"
The leader shares the story starter with the players, who then form small groups. Each group creates the rest of the story and rehearses their idea. Prior to playing, however, each group uses found sounds to improvise an interlude (music between scenes) that foreshadows their ending. When it is their turn, they play their interlude and then share their dramatization with classmates.

"Winter Fun"
Snow has been falling all night, and the ground is covered with a glistening blanket. You and your friends decide to go sledding. You get your sled from the garage and pull it behind you as you walk quickly to the park to meet your friends. You hardly notice the cold as you look down the hill and try to see what course you will take. Then your friends . . .

After each group has shared their story, invite the players to sit in a circle and imagine that they are sitting in front of a fireplace and drinking hot cocoa after their day of outdoor fun. Not only does this provide an additional opportunity to use their imaginations, it also serves as a quieting activity.

Story Creation from Improvisation: "Protection Money"
Give players the following scenario, and ask them to create a story about how Pete can get Eric to stop bullying him. Challenge them to create a peaceful solution to the problem; no violence should be used. Players may add characters if desired, and volunteers can be invited to play their stories for classmates.

Who: Eric and Pete.
What: Every day, Eric forces Pete to give up his lunch money. He tells Pete that it is "protection money," as paying will protect Pete from being hurt. Pete is afraid of Eric; he is small in stature and Eric is a big bully.
Where: The playground.

After players share their stories either orally or through play, engage them in a discussion about conflict resolution. Ask them to respond to the question, "Does might always make right?" and encourage them to identify characters from literature or historical figures who have used peaceful means to solve problems.

Ensemble Singing and Improvisation: "If I Had a Hammer"

The leader rehearses the song "If I Had a Hammer," giving attention to the objects (hammer, bell, song) that lend themselves to improvisation within the song. Players suggest other objects that could be incorporated into the lyrics to provide potential for sound, movement, or dramatization—for example, "If I had a book, I'd read it in the morning"; "If I had a bike, I'd ride it in the morning"; and so on. Players discuss ways the "character" of the object or experience can be expressed through select expression of sound and gesture.

ASSESSMENT: Complete the rubric shown in table 6.1.

Table 6.1. Rubric for Sample Lesson

	Yes	No	In part
Players conveyed meaning through characters, environment, and actions.			
Players musically supported the story.			
Players demonstrated an understanding of plot, characters, theme, and setting.			

CHAPTER 7

Integrating Creative Choices

You have been progressing from simple to complex activities in the journey toward mastering essentials in creative drama and music. You are now ready for the most complex and challenging activities the two forms offer. In this chapter, you will incorporate previous learning into stories and sounds that are at the apex of the creative process.

You will want to allow adequate time for exploration and integration. These are activities that foster an appreciation for good stories; motivate players to improve reading, listening, and communication skills; and help develop sequencing skills. They provide opportunities for employing critical thinking; increasing empathy; promoting teamwork and cooperation; and increasing awareness of dramatic, literary, and musical structure. Players gain practice in identifying what makes a good story, a good dramatization, and a good composition.

Story dramatization, accompaniment, and composition require players to use both skill and imagination. They will develop content, characters, and compositions that bring it all together.

STORY DRAMATIZATION (LOWER/UPPER LEVELS)

Story dramatization, bringing stories to life through words and actions, is the most complex of all creative drama activities. In preparing for story dramatization, players should demonstrate competence in the areas below.

- concentrating
- ensemble playing
- using imagination
- physically portraying characters
- finding a character's voice
- creating dialogue
- understanding story structure
- creating believable characters

Nowhere is creative drama's link to literature more obvious or important than in story dramatization. Here players face challenges, move forward or backward in history, meet characters who are either like or unlike them, and experience different cultures and customs. Each story dramatization can be a new adventure that is either integrated into the curriculum or enjoyed on its own merits.

The process is one of breaking a story down into small units, working through each unit, and building the story back up again by combining each section. Replaying is essential, and each subsequent playing of a segment should clarify or enrich it. **Evaluation** further deepens involvement and understanding, adds dimension to characterization, and helps structure the plot.

Story dramatization is a precursor to more formal theatre experience. Casting is individual, with one player per role. Opportunities exist, however, to involve the entire group when trying on characters or replaying.

Story dramatization offers flexibility. Players may be interested in an entire story or only in one or a few scenes. Options include dramatizing (1) critical or favorite scenes; (2) a new scene that follows the story's written conclusion; (3) one that serves as exposition (an **expository scene**); or (4) something that is suggested or touched upon briefly in the story but is not well developed.

The story dramatization process can be completed in one session or over time. Regardless of the number of scenes played, this activity should not be rushed. Continue working only as long as the process is productive and the players remain interested.

To successfully dramatize a story requires comprehension of its basic elements. Players will need to understand the plot, characters, setting, and climax of a story. Reading or hearing it more than once may be helpful.

When introducing the story, the leader should strive to motivate the players and focus their attention. Introductions should be long enough to pique curiosity and gain attention without overshadowing the story itself.

Telling a story well contributes to successful playing. It is difficult for players to be receptive to a story if they think that the leader doesn't like it. Expressiveness enriches the narrative. Checking for comprehension and attentive behaviors through eye contact and questions helps build rapport. For best results, the leader should learn the story in ideas rather than specific words. Practice will improve delivery.

The Story Dramatization Process
The actual dramatization follows a basic procedure. Experienced leaders may adapt the process to reflect personal style. Until the leader is comfortable with story dramatization, however, following this format is recommended.

STEPS IN STORY DRAMATIZATION

- tell story
- general discussion
- specific discussion
- try-on
- try-on (pairs or groups)
- plan
- play
- evaluate
- replay
- continue as described

1. *Tell the story.*
2. Lead the players in a *general discussion* focusing on major plot developments and the important characters. This general discussion usually involves asking players to recap the story in their own words. This accomplishes two important things. First, by listening to players

as they retell the story, the leader can check for comprehension. Second, if some players have missed important points, content can be reviewed. Players will feel awkward and uncomfortable later in the process if they are unclear about what happens in the story. This general discussion is intended to solidify information for players. Listing responses on the board is recommended.

3. A *specific discussion* now more narrowly focuses on the number of scenes, where these begin and end, and the critical action within each. Players should determine scenic divisions. Opinions may differ as to how to segment the story, and the leader's task is to help the players arrive at consensus. Not all classes will divide a story in exactly the same way, but if the units make sense and encompass the key points and characters in the story, they are acceptable. In the story example that follows, players have identified three to six scenes for play.

In any discussion or evaluation, the leader should ask open-ended questions to stimulate creative thinking. Players, for example, may wish to create their own expository scene. Or they may wish to develop a scene not found in the story.

4. Conduct a **try-on** of major characters. Here, everyone assumes the same role, showing the character engaged in some action. Whether or not the action is found in the story, it should suit the character.

Typically, this step begins with characters in the first scene and is done in unison. The leader asks the players to identify the main characters in the scene, close their eyes, and envision the first character. Players are asked to signal that they have an image by raising their hands. When everyone has an idea, players should lower their hands and open their eyes. Each player then tells one thing about the character as envisioned. This try-on provides everyone with an opportunity to imagine the character and lets the leader check for understanding.

Example 1:

Leader: Who are the major characters in the first scene?

Player 1: Becky and Jayna.

Leader: Good. Please stand in a circle and close your eyes. Imagine Becky. When you see her clearly in your imagination, raise your hand so I know that you are ready.

(Players form a circle, close their eyes, raise their hands.)

Leader: All right. Open your eyes now, and lower your hands. Let's go around the circle and have each of you tell one thing about your Becky.

Player 1: She's blonde.

Player 2: She's short.

Player 3: She's tall.

Player 4: She's wearing jeans.

It does not matter if players have the same image of the characters; what counts is that each player has an image. The leader should accept all answers that demonstrate focused thinking.

The next portion of this try-on is played in pantomime and in unison. Players use as much room as needed for this and return to their places when their try-ons are complete. This gives the leader an opportunity to observe all initial interpretations.

Example 2:

Leader: In pantomime and using as much space as needed, show me your

Becky as she talks on the phone to her friend. Return to your place when finished.

Repeat the process described in example 1 for Jayna. When players have an image of the character, they can try her on as in example 3.

Example 3:

Leader: In pantomime and using as much space as needed, show me your Jayna window-shopping at the mall. Return to your place when finished.

In example 2, players use action found in the story to try on the role of Becky. In example 3, the action is suggested by the story and is logical for the character. As story dramatization work progresses, all characters can be tried on this way.

5. Next, characters can be *paired or grouped for a new try-on*. This is played in unison. Dialogue is usually incorporated here. Before try-on begins, the leader should ask for examples of things that the characters might say. This try-on may be noisy! When players have completed this try-on, they return to their space. The leader then asks them to share what their characters said or did. Roles can be reversed for replay so that each player is acquainted with more than one character.

Example 4:

Leader: Select a partner. Decide which role each of you will play. Show me Becky and Jayna riding the bus to the mall. What might they say to each other? When you've completed your try-on, return to your place.

6. It is now time to *plan* the first scene. This segment begins with reviewing where the scene begins and ends and the action within it. The scene can be done in pantomime or with dialogue. This is also the time to establish the physical setting, putting tables, chairs, and so on in the playing space as needed.

Casting is at the leader's discretion and places one person in each role. This is called *individual play*. Some leaders prefer to cast stronger players initially to increase chances for success; other leaders prefer to cast from volunteers.

7. *Playing the scene* comes next, and the cast moves into the setting. The leader may wish to make a few comments related to the mood of the scene. Action can be cued with "curtain" to begin and "freeze" to stop. The scene is then dramatized.

8. *Evaluation* follows playing and focuses on what the players did well, what might be improved, and what changes the players might want to make. This critique should begin by drawing attention to what went well and why. Open-ended questions help move players beyond "I liked it" or "I didn't like it," and encourage insightful reactions. Comments should be addressed to characters rather than players, as talking about what a character did or said removes some of the onus from a flawed or poorly developed scene. Leaders should model evaluation from a respectful and critical point of view.

9. *Replay* follows evaluation. The purpose is to incorporate suggestions for improving play, to cast other players, or to try new ideas or interpretations. The original cast can replay if desired. Evaluation should take place after each replaying, and the pattern of replay-evaluate-replay

should continue until the scene is satisfactory.

10. *Continue.* Each scene in a story should be developed this way, starting with step 3 when more than one scene will be dramatized in a session. Completed scenes should be joined together until the entire story can be told through dramatization.

While creative drama is process oriented rather than performance oriented, story dramatization may resemble a theatre piece in several ways. Replays, for example, might be thought of as rehearsals. The leader should remember that initial playings can be superficial, but replaying truly develops scenes. While creative drama can be done without costumes and props, using them may inspire characterization. Lights can be dimmed or music used for mood. Creative drama requires none of these, but can integrate them. The process is player-centered rather than audience-centered, and public performance is not a goal. If, however, players wish to share their completed dramatizations, the request may indicate their pride and enjoyment.

Story Dramatization Activity: "Jayna's Dilemma"

Jayna always liked going shopping with Becky. The two girls could spend hours in the mall going from store to store, trying on clothes and jewelry. They enjoyed imagining what it would be like to have money to buy all of the things they wanted. The two young friends, however, usually found that bus fare to the mall and a pretzel and cola once inside were all that they could afford.

One day Becky called Jayna. "My cousin is in town. She's visiting me for a few days and she wants to go shopping. Do you want to come? She has a car and she'll drive us," Becky said excitedly.

"Great," said Jayna. "Come and get me."

Becky's cousin, Bonnie, was a pretty girl of sixteen. She drove a red sports car. During the ride to the mall, the two younger girls could barely sit still. They were so impressed by Bonnie's car, her expensive clothes, and her stories of parties and dates that they could hardly conceal their admiration.

Once inside the mall, the three girls went to a department store. They stood looking for a long time at the jewelry on display. "I would love to have these earrings," said Jayna as she held a pair to her face and looked at herself in the mirror.

"They look great on you," said Becky.

"My birthday is next week. Maybe someone will get them for me as a present," Jayna sighed. "I can't afford them."

The girls were silent for a moment as Jayna placed the earrings on top of the display counter. Then Bonnie said, "If you want them, I'll get them for you."

Jayna was elated. Bonnie opened her wallet, but instead of taking out money to pay for the earrings, she looked around carefully. Seeing no salesperson, she dropped the earrings into her wallet. "Let's go," she said, and the three girls left the store and went home.

All that night, Jayna felt confused. She had gotten the earrings she wanted, but she wasn't enjoying them. Jayna's stomach hurt and she could hardly eat dinner. Later, she called Becky and they had a long talk.

Early the next morning, Jayna and Becky took the bus to the mall. They went to the department store and Jayna asked a clerk if she could speak to the manager. Mr. Thomas, the manager of the jewelry department, smiled as he introduced himself to the girls. "What can I do for you?" he asked.

Becky held the earrings in her hand while Jayna explained. "I was given these earrings as a gift, but no one paid for them. I can't keep them." Mr. Thomas took the earrings. He thanked the girls and returned the jewelry to its rightful place. As Becky and Jayna started to leave, he called to them. "You did the right thing, you know. I am proud that two such honest and responsible young ladies shop in my store." Jayna smiled at Becky. "Thanks for coming with me," she said quietly. Becky hugged her.

The girls decided to spend the rest of the morning window shopping and to buy themselves a pretzel and a cola. As they looked at the store displays, they realized that shopping without Bonnie was a lot more fun.

ACCOMPANIMENT
(LOWER/UPPER LEVELS)

Most music that serves as accompaniment enhances the mood and supports the action of the story. If something exciting occurs, for instance, the music may reflect that by increasing the tempo, intensity, dynamics, or melodic direction. With tension in the story, the accompaniment might add dissonant harmony. On the other hand, some accompaniment for a "they lived happily ever after" story would be tranquil and consonant. Players have opportunities to build the mood and convey the action by creatively adjusting these elements when they know the story well.

Accompaniment, then, is essentially a background figure in the process of storytelling. Players must recognize early that their accompaniment contributions are secondary, not center stage. Without diminishing the role of accompaniment,

players will have to acquire sensitivity and learn to be "team players" in collaborative performance. They should channel their creativity into devising musical thoughts that are more subtle and supportive. Whether the accompaniment is for a story, poem, or dance, it should support, not compete with, the main attraction.

The style of accompaniment must be considered carefully. It is composed rather than improvised. The choice of instruments or sounds needs to be based on what type of effect is desired. This usually involves consulting with the performers. It curtails the amount of freedom in spinning out spontaneous material and demands more attention to timed events in the dramatization. Musical elements such as the **texture**, dynamics, and intensity of the accompaniment will need to be closely aligned to the story actions—always accompanying, not predicting or following, dramatic events. The players who accompany must have a clear idea of the sequence in a story, poem, or dance.

Music has a significant role in contributing to storytelling. Many plays, movies, and television programs are enhanced by appropriate music that accompanies the story line. To raise awareness of its role, players might listen to music on a television program without watching the set and determine what might be happening in the story. This exercise heightens sensitivity to the function of accompaniment and serves as an interesting discussion point to underscore its purpose.

Television programming is not the only form that deserves accompaniment. Chants, rhymes, dance, poems, and children's stories can also be enhanced this way. The sequence of activities that follow players from some simple, familiar experiences to highly sophisticated and abstract ones. Previous activities (such as improvising, movement, and word painting) help build players' confidence.

One simple accompaniment activity is the **leitmotif**. A common practice in accompanying stories or poems is to assign a particular sound, such as a short melodic fragment or rhythmic pattern, to a central character in the story. Operatic composers use the leitmotif technique when specific characters appear and reappear on stage or when characters are referred to throughout the drama. Players may create leitmotifs and experiment with this technique using simple nursery rhymes. Instruments (e.g., resonator bells) or body sounds (e.g., snapping fingers, patchen) can be used for initial experiences.

Take, for instance, "Mary Had a Little Lamb." Begin the activity by dividing the players into two groups. Assign some players to chant the rhyme; assign others to perform a motif each time Mary (or reference to her) appears. Practice reciting the rhyme with all players, to familiarize them with it.

Distribute the G and E resonator bells to several players and practice the suggested leitmotif below.

Example:
Leitmotif for Mary:

Figure 7.1

Directions: While some players chant, players perform the motif (as illustrated with the X which follows).

   X
Mary had a little lamb,
Little lamb, little lamb.
   X
Mary had a little lamb,
Its fleece was white as snow.
            X
And everywhere that Mary went,
  X   X
Mary went, Mary went,
           X
Ev'ry where that Mary went,
The lamb was sure to go.
      X
It followed her to school one day,
School one day, school one day, etc.

Stories such as those of Pinocchio, Snow White and the Seven Dwarfs, and the Three Pigs lend themselves to leitmotifs. A more colorful palette of sound sources for leitmotifs can include found sounds and vocal sounds. The leader should encourage players to be resourceful and discriminating in their selection of sounds. Once accompanists develop skill with the leitmotifs, they can branch out to develop more complete accompaniments. While the leader needs to be certain to select a story that has plenty of potential for creative accompaniment, the players must avoid the temptation to accompany minor characters and events. Experimentation, imitation, and refinement are necessary.

COMPOSITION (UPPER LEVEL)

Professional composers often "hear" their music internally before they write their **scores**. They know what melodies, rhythms, instruments, and so forth will be part of the composition before notes are placed on score paper. Players also have the aptitude to compose, in that they can draw what they hear inside their heads. Even when they do not have the technical skills of note reading, they have the musical skills of inner hearing, imaginative listening, and drawing. Before players take on the task of composing, it is suggested that scoring or mapping may whet their appetites. The composition process may take four or five sessions to adequately prepare players.

Precomposition:
Mapping and Scoring

Occasionally, young players may ask to sing a song for the class. The leader might seize the opportunity to "map" or score the song as the player sings it again the same way. For instance, the leader may draw the melodic direction, indicate the rhythmic pattern, or show the articulation (e.g., pitches detached or smoothly connected). The following example illustrates different mapping techniques to score the elements of music:

> Melodic direction mapping (figure 7.2).
> Rhythm pattern notation (figure 7.3).
> Articulation (figure 7.4).

Following the leader's example, players will be ready to map their music. To start, it is recommended that they practice mapping familiar songs or recorded music. The melody of "The Star-Spangled Banner," the rhythm to "Happy Birthday" and the articulation of "Chim Chim Cher-ee" are recommended for practice. See the list of familiar songs in chapter 2 for other suggestions.

With recorded music, almost any band or orchestral composition will work;

[Melodic Direction Mapping]

Figure 7.2

however, it should be short and have powerful rhythmic and melodic interest. The first session should introduce the task of listening to the music only. To avoid distractions, players close their eyes and listen to the "story." Invite players to feel the mood and respond to its affective potential.

Upon second listening, players begin to focus on the orchestral sounds. Using mural-sized paper (at least three feet by twelve feet), players prepare to draw what is happening in the music (not the story line). They listen carefully to certain types of instruments, such as wind, string, or percussion. Music that has clear instrumentation is optimal (such as "Mars" from Gustav Holst's *Planets*, "In the Hall of the Mountain King" from Edvard Grieg's *Peer Gynt* Suite, or "Sirenes" from Claude Debussy's *La mer*). Then the leader breaks the listening down into smaller temporal units, assigning some players to draw the opening section, and others to draw the middle and ending sections. Once the music changes, the players will need to draw these changes in the melody, rhythm, harmony, dynamics, and texture.

If players have had experience keeping a sound journal (chapter 3), they have

[Rhythm Pattern Notation]

— — —— — — —— — — —— —— ——   **Figure 7.3**

[Articulation]

Figure 7.4

already devised some notation schemes for sounds. The mural score, however, has many more dimensions than a map. Players can critique their choices of color, thickness of line, contour of line, proportion of drawings, texture of the composition, and overall mood. The leader prompts analysis through questions. For example, "How do your scores portray solo sections? How do the scores illustrate loud passages, dissonant harmonies, and melodic phrases?" Since this activity involves listening to many aural events and devising abstract symbols, there is plenty of room for creative responses. The players will wish to listen and re-listen to the music often.

From the mural experience, the leader can point out effective mapping devices (swirls, arrows, colors, etc.) that can later be used in composition scores. For example, the mural may have small pastel, upward-moving, swirling clouds or large, bold, pointy, downward black arrows. Each of these notations stands for a different sound and communicates a different performance effect.

Mural scores are never precise representations of what occurred in the music. The notation, however, does tell the listener some things about the characteristics of the sounds. Inasmuch as the mural activity allows, players will get across what they hear and feel and discuss one another's creative symbols. They seldom tire of the mural activity when good music has

been chosen and the experience allows them to express a variety of music.

Notating Compositions, Level 1
Activities such as mapping and scoring lead to other types of composition. Players who have had plenty of experience improvising will soon yearn to "save" their creative work. The need arises for them to remember it from day to day or from person to person. Though technology can always record extemporaneous work and software can prepare musical scores, players can derive a great deal of satisfaction in writing down their creative work—even if they are not trained in standard musical notation. Because players will have had several discussions that detail the elements of music, they already have a general understanding of pitch level, rhythm, harmony, tone color, form, and dynamics.

Any of the musical games in chapters 2 through 6 can be scored, that is, written down, for future use. The composer must make some choices as to how each sound source (body sound, found/environmental sound, or instrumental sound) will be represented. The leader constructively contributes to composition activities by questioning the players' notation choices. For example, if a sound is to be repeated rapidly, the leader can ask, "How can you illustrate the sound so it appears the way we hear it?" The composer's challenge is to communicate in such a way that others will be able to understand the sound's characteristics.

Notating Compositions, Level 2
Moving scores to a performance level requires more group planning and discussion. First, determine the number of players and sound sources. Second, create a score large enough for all to read. Third, invite the composer to conduct and monitor the performance. Fourth, title the composition.

Example: Trio Talk

In the composition shown in figure 7.5, the composer envisioned the piece as performed by three players. Player 1 uses body sounds (clapping and patchen). Player 2 uses found sounds (tapping the window with a pencil). Player 3 has bottles (one pitched high, one medium, and one low) and a spoon. The composer created the piece in triple meter, that is, beats were grouped in sets of three. The patterns for Players 1 and 2 synchronize on the beat. The volume changes with the patchen and window taps, according to the change in size of notation. Player 3 performs the high to medium to low tones by gently swishing the bottles with a spoon. The composer provides the starting tempo and gives players gestures that will help them start together and perform the piece in the intended manner.

Two secondary activities often result from these performances: (1) Composers wish to revise their compositions once they hear them. They get better ideas on the spot, and they should be encouraged to edit. (2) The players are challenged by the notational systems and may suggest alternative symbols. For the best results, allow plenty of time for these follow-up activities.

A FINAL WORD
The activities in this chapter have offered opportunities for creative exploration, adaptation, and artistry. The leader and players now have graduated to experiences with complex creative drama and music processes. The final stage in combining creative choices is to bring together story dramatization, accompaniment, and composition. Dramatizing stories (either published or original) and

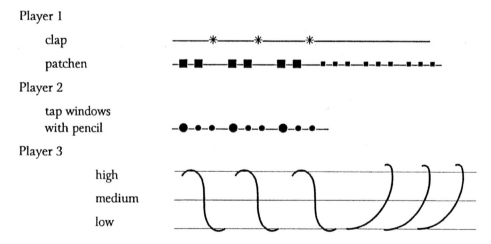

Figure 7.5

enhancing them with musical support integrates artistic processes. The creative growth and artistic development of the players—the heart of the experiences in this book—is at its zenith in these activities. Enjoy!

SOME SUGGESTED STORIES TO DRAMATIZE

Many favorite children's stories can be dramatized. Some titles are listed below. A children's reference librarian can be helpful in locating literature. Players also enjoy dramatizing stories that they are reading.

Aardema, Verna. *Why Mosquitoes Buzz in People's Ears: A West African Tale*. New York: Dial Books, 1975.

Allard, Harry. *Miss Nelson Is Missing*. New York: Houghton Mifflin, 1977.

Andersen, Hans Christian. *The Emperor's New Clothes*. New York: Houghton Mifflin, 1977.

Chase, Richard. *The Jack Tales*. New York: Houghton Mifflin, 1971.

Cherry, Lynne. *The Great Kapok Tree: A Tale of the Amazon Rain Forest*. San Diego: Harcourt Brace Jovanovich, 1990.

Collodi, Carlo. *The Adventures of Pinocchio*. Mineola, N.Y.: Dover, 1995.

Cooney, Barbara. *Miss Rumphius*. New York: Penguin Puffin Books, 1982.

Dahl, Roald. *Charlie and the Chocolate Factory*. New York: Knopf, 1964.

————. *James and the Giant Peach*. New York: Penguin Puffin Books, 1996.

DePaola, Tomie. *Strega Nona: An Old Tale*. New York: Aladdin, 1975.

Dorros, Arthur. *Abuela*. New York: Penguin Puffin Books, 1991.

Eastman, Phillip D. *Are You My Mother?* New York: Random House, 1960.

Flack, Marjorie. *Ask Mr. Bear*. New York: Simon and Schuster Children's Publishing, 1971.

Fox, Mem. *Wilfred Gordon McDonald Partridge*. La Jolla, Calif.: Kane/Miller, 1984.

Galdone, Paul. *Magic Porridge Pot*. New York: Clarion Books, 1976.

Garcia, Maria. *The Adventures of Connie and Diego*. San Francisco: Children's Book Press, 1997.

Greenfield, Eloise. *Nathaniel Talking*. New York: Black Butterfly Children's Books, 1988.

Grimes, Nikki. *Meet Danitra Brown*. New York: HarperCollins, 1997.

Grimm, Jacob. *The Bremen Town Musicians*. New York: North-South Books, 1997.

Hamilton, Virginia. *The People Could Fly: American Black Folktales*. New York: Knopf Books for Young Readers, 1993.

Herrera, Juan Felipe. *The Upside Down Boy*. San Francisco: Children's Book Press, 2000.

Hume, Lotta Carswell. *Favorite Children's Stories from China and Tibet*. North Clarendon, Vt.: Tuttle, 1989.

Jacobs, Joseph. *English Fairy Tales, Collected by Joseph Jacobs*. N.p., Seven Treasures, 2008.

Johnson, Crockett. *Harold and the Purple Crayon*. New York: HarperCollins, 1998.

Keats, Ezra Jack. *The Snowy Day*. New York: Viking, 1962.

Kipling, Rudyard. *The Elephant's Child*. Orlando: Voyager Books, 1983.

Lester, Julius. *John Henry*. New York: Puffin Books, 1994.

Lionni, Leo. *Frederick*. New York: Dragonfly Books, 1967.

Lowry, Lois. *Gooney Bird Greene*. New York: Yearling, 2004.

Marshall, James. *The Three Little Pigs*. New York: Dial Books for Young Readers, 1989.

Martin, Rafe. *The Rough-Face Girl*. New York: Putnam Juvenile, 1998.

McGovern, Ann. *Stone Soup*. New York: Scholastic, 1986.

McKissack, Patricia C. *Mirandy and Brother Wind*. New York: Dragonfly Books, 1996.

Mora, Pat. *Tomas and the Library Lady*. New York: Dragonfly Books, 2000.

Polacco, Patricia. *Mrs. Katz and Tush*. New York: Bantam Doubleday Dell Books for Young Readers, 1994.

Sakai, Kimiko. *Sachiko Means Happiness*. San Francisco: Children's Book Press, 1997.

San Souci, Robert D. *The Talking Eggs*. New York: Dial Books for Young Readers, 1989.

Scheer, George F., ed. *Cherokee Animal Tales*. Tulsa, Okla.: Council Oak Books, 2006.

Sendak, Maurice. *Where the Wild Things Are*. New York: HarperCollins, 1988.

Dr. Seuss. *The Cat in the Hat*. New York: Random House Books for Young Readers, 1957.

————. *The Lorax*. New York: Random House, 1971.

Silverstein, Shel. *A Light in the Attic*. New York: HarperCollins, 1981.

————. *Where the Sidewalk Ends: The Poems and Drawings of Shel Silverstein*. New York: HarperCollins, 1974.

Slobodkina, Esphyr. *Caps for Sale*. New York: HarperCollins, 1987.

Soto, Gary. *The Old Man and His Door*. New York: Putnam Juvenile, 1998.

————. *Too Many Tamales*. New York: Putnam Juvenile, 1996.

Steptoe, John. *Mufaro's Beautiful Daughters*. New York: HarperCollins, 1987.

Stevens, Janet. The Three Billy Goats Gruff. Orlando: Harcourt Brace, 1987.

Tolstoy, Aleksey Nikolayevich. *Great Big Enormous Turnip*. New York: F. Watts, 1968.

Viorst, Judith. *Alexander and the Terrible, Horrible, No Good, Very Bad Day*. New York: Atheneum, 1987.

Waber, Bernard. *Ira Sleeps Over*. Boston: Houghton Mifflin, 1972.

Watts, Bernadette, and Aesop. *The Lion and the Mouse*. New York: North-South Books, 2007.

White, E. B. *Charlotte's Web*. New York: HarperCollins, 2001.

Wilder, Laura Ingalls. *The Little House on the Prairie*. New York: HarperCollins, 2008.

Xiong, Blia. *Nine-in-One GRR! GRR!* San Francisco: Children's Book Press, 1997.

Yep, Laurence. *The Rainbow People*. New York: HarperCollins, 1989.

Young, Ed. *Lon Po Po*. New York: Putnam Juvenile, 1996.

Zemach, Margot. *The Three Wishes*. New York: Farrar, Straus and Giroux, 1993.

SAMPLE LESSON, CHAPTER 7

LESSON OVERVIEW: This lesson illustrates how creative drama and music activities can be united through story dramatization. The adapted story is inspired by a folk tale about hospitality and generosity.

RECOMMENDED GRADES: 7 and 8

CONTENT AREAS: drama/theatre, music, reading, and language arts

INSTRUCTIONAL OBJECTIVES:

- Players explore characters, plot, theme, and setting. (Reading and language arts)
- Players create scenes based upon literature. (Drama/theatre)
- Players compose short pieces within specified guidelines. (Music)

LENGTH OF LESSON: forty-five to sixty minutes.

ACTIVITIES AND PROCEDURES:

Preparation: Review the characteristics of a folk tale with the players before engaging in the following activities.

Story Dramatization with Accompaniment: "The Generous Hosts"

Coming from an oral tradition, folk tales can be found in countries around the world. With their interesting characters, explanations of natural events, or universal lessons, they often make good material to dramatize. In this lesson, players first read the story. Next, they form several large groups. In a class of thirty students, for example, there may be three groups of ten. Each group then divides in half, with one set of players working on a story dramatization and the other composing an accompaniment.

Players decide whether to give a character or object a particular accompaniment figure, such as a leitmotif. After determining whether the story should build in dynamics, tempo, and/or texture, the accompanists work closely with the players who dramatize the story, so that the accompaniment is performed in close coordination with the meaning. After the first combined practice, the accompanists decide if the story would be enhanced by a brief overture and coda. When both subgroups have completed their work, the story should be performed with accompaniment.

"The Generous Hosts"

In a village lived a poor peasant and his wife. They did not have much, but they were generous people and always willing to share their meager possessions.

One day, as the man and his wife were sitting down to dinner, there came a knock at their door. The man answered it to find his neighbor standing there. "Friend," said the neighbor, "I was in my yard when I smelled the most wonderful aroma coming from your house. I had to see for myself the source of this magnificent smell." The peasant said, "We are having a stew of chicken, noodles, and vegetables. Won't you join us?" The neighbor was delighted and the three of them sat down to a delicious dinner.

When the meal was over and the neighbor had gone home, the wife said, "Husband, that meal was to feed us for a week. Now we only have enough left over for a few days." The husband said, "We could not turn away our neighbor." The wife agreed.

The next day, just as the peasant and his wife were sitting down to dinner, there came a knock on the door. The wife opened the door to find the neighbor standing there. "Good woman," said the neighbor, "I could not stop thinking about the delicious meal we shared yesterday." "Come in," said the wife. "We have some remaining." The husband fetched another plate and divided the meal intended for two into three portions.

When the meal was over and the neighbor had gone home, the husband said, "Wife, that meal was to feed us for a few days. Now we have very little left." The wife said, "We could not turn away our neighbor." The husband agreed.

One the third day, just as the peasant and his wife were sitting down to dinner, there came a knock on the door. The husband and the wife went to the door to find the neighbor standing there. "Friends," said the neighbor, "I could not stop thinking about the wonderful meals we have shared." "Come in," said the husband. The wife fetched another plate and divided the stew into three portions. It amounted to a spoonful for each of them. The neighbor looked with disdain upon the meager meal, ate his share in one bite, and went home.

The next day, the peasant and his wife sat down to dinner. They had only some broth remaining from the previous meals, but they were content. They anticipated a knock at the door, but it did not come. This time, they ate alone. The neighbor, knowing that their generosity had been exhausted, found somewhere else to dine.

ASSESSMENT: Complete the rubric shown in table 7.1.

Table 7.1. Rubric for Sample Lesson

	Yes	No	In part
Players used imagination in story creation.			
Players used imagination to create accompainment.			
Players used voice expressively.			
Players created an interlude that foreshadowed an event in a story.			
Players learned and contributed productively as individuals and as members of groups.			

Sample Lesson

MANY OF THE ACTIVITIES IN THIS BOOK can be used in conjunction with a variety of content areas. Opportunities abound for planning lessons in which creative drama and music are integrated with a unit of study in social studies, science, math, language arts, or some other field. The following unit offers a viable format for such lessons, including ideas for leader's comments.

RECOMMENDED GRADE: 3
TITLE/THEME OF UNIT: Australia
CONTENT AREAS: drama/theatre, music, geography, and language arts

INSTRUCTIONAL OBJECTIVES:
- Players will understand Australia's physical and human characteristics. (Geography)
- Players will express and interpret information and ideas. (Language arts)
- Players will use research to support classroom dramatizations. (Drama/theatre).
- Players will imagine and describe characters through movement and voice. (Drama/theatre)
- Players will sing or accompany to express musical ideas. (Music)
- Players will improvise using traditional and nontraditional sound sources. (Music)

LENGTH OF LESSONS: Two sessions of forty-five to sixty minutes each.

ACTIVITIES AND PROCEDURES:
Preparation: This unit builds on research assignments on the continent's location, natural resources, climate, and topographical features.
MATERIALS: boomerang and art supplies

LEADER'S INTRODUCTION

Yesterday your assignment was to find interesting information on the people and land of Australia. Today we will build upon that homework. Who can tell me another name for Australia? (Players respond.) That's right. It's called the land "Down Under." (Leader holds up a boomerang for students to see.) Who knows what this is? (Players respond.) Right. It's a boomerang. The indigenous people used these to hunt. Today we're going to continue our exploration of the land "Down Under." (Players and leader sit in a circle on the floor.)

ACTIVITIES

Circle Game: I'm Going to Australia, and I'm Going to See . . .

Leader: We'll begin our journey with the activity "I'm Going to Australia, and I'm Going to See . . ." I'll name the first item. We'll go around the circle with each of you naming what we'd see or experience in Australia and then adding something of your own.

Leader: I'm going to Australia, and I'm going to see Ayers Rock.

Player 1: I'm going to Australia, and I'm going to see Ayers Rock and a sheep station.

Player 2: I'm going to Australia, and I'm going to see Ayers Rock, a sheep station, and an opal miner.

(The game continues.)

Leader: You've identified a lot of information about Australia that will help us in our dramatic work. Knowing about people, places, and events makes our dramatic interpretations more believable.

Pantomime Sentences: Australian Animals

Leader: Let's see what we can remember about the animals of Australia. Instead of telling me, I'd like you to show me how each animal moves in these pantomime sentences. Find plenty of personal space and use your body to portray the animal.

You are a koala sucking on a gum leaf. (Sidecoaching: Some of you look so drowsy.)

You are a kangaroo hopping on your powerful hind legs. (Sidecoaching: How high can you hop? I see some of you have joeys in your pouches.)

You are a dingo stalking your prey. (Sidecoaching: What do you like to eat? How is your movement different from a pet dog's?)

You are an emu running quickly across the ground. (Sidecoaching: Remember, an emu can't fly. How quickly can you run?)

You are a kookaburra flying in the sky, landing in a tree, and laughing your unique laugh. (Sidecoaching: How can you show, in pantomime, that you are laughing?)

You are a Tasmanian devil showing off your fierce teeth. (Sidecoaching: You certainly look dangerous with your big head and sharp teeth.)

You are a wombat burrowing. (Sidecoaching: How deeply will you dig?)

Leader: What are some of the fundamental movements we used to portray these animals? (Players respond.) Imagining the character and variations in our movements helps us to develop believable characterizations.

Ensemble Singing: Australian Animals Get Caught

Leader: Do you remember the old song "Charlie over the Ocean"? Let's create some new lyrics for that song and substitute what might be caught in Australia. But first, let's select a new name for the bloke. Charlie isn't necessarily an Australian name. Who has an idea? (Players offer suggestions.) Now, which sea or seas would our chap be crossing? (Players respond and refer to maps or globe.)

I'm going to give you some thinking time. Prepare to sing your animal (or item) when I point to you in the song. In case someone else sings your idea, let's each have two answers in mind.

The leader sings the tune "Charlie over the Ocean," substituting the name of a player and inserting "wombat" for the first animal.

The leader points to Ian and sings:

Ian over the ocean, (players repeat)
Ian over the sea, (players repeat)
Ian caught a *wombat*, (players repeat)
Didn't catch me. (players repeat)

On subsequent verses the leader points to individual players, who sing their responses at the point marked with asterisks.

Accompaniment: Australian Instruments

Guitars and banjos are often used in Australian folk music. Only one chord is needed if the leader or players are to accompany the "Charlie" tune on these instruments. Simply strum a C chord to the beat. If no guitar or banjo is available, an Autoharp serves as the nearest cousin.

Improvisation: Natural Resources

Leader: We've been learning about the strange and wonderful natural resources in Australia. The country has an interesting terrain. What do I mean by terrain? (Players respond.)

What are some of the unique aspects of a billabong? How might it look in the spring? In the winter? (Players respond.)

Leader: We will have to find sounds to tell the state of the billabong or describe the natural resources. Let's use what we know about the landmarks and natural resources to improvise a billabong or describe the natural resources.

The leader divides students into teams of four to six players and provides direction on the length of the sound piece: it is to last two minutes. After five to ten minutes of practice and discussion, players perform their improvisations.

Leader: As these sound pieces are performed, we listeners will determine why the piece was titled the way it was. Listen for clues.

Story Creation: "Australian School Day (circa 1850s)"

Leader: Now, think about your typical school day. What subjects do we study? What else do we do? If you were an Australian pupil in the 1850s, your school day would be quite different.

You have already researched a typical school day in an Australian school during the mid-nineteenth century. Let's review what we have found.

"A Mid-Nineteenth Century Australian School Day"[1]
The following information is provided to assist the teacher.

Typical content studied:

reading
multiplication tables
writing, spelling, diction
grammar
geography
singing
drawing (for boys)
sewing (for girls)

Rules of behavior:

Boys and girls sit on separate sides of the room and walk in separate lines behind the teacher.
Girls enter and exit rooms before boys do.
Hats are always worn out of doors. Boys remove caps when they enter a room and when they meet a lady.
When in the company of adults, children must have permission to speak or be spoken to first.
Children's arms and legs must be completely covered by clothing, and girls cannot show bare ankles.
Writing with the left hand is not permitted.
Children must always sit straight.

In the classroom:

Chairs do not have backs.
Children are inspected for cleanliness.
The teacher may be quite strict.
The teacher may be financially penalized if an inspector finds the classroom or the students lacking.

Using this information, work in small groups. Create and dramatize a story based on the following first line:

Today is a special day at school because an important visitor is coming.

(Players create, rehearse, play, and evaluate the stories.)

Leader: You were very inventive with your stories and developed interesting characters. Now, let's do a quieting activity.

Quieting Activity: The Crocodile

Leader: You are a crocodile sunning yourself on the banks of a billabong.

Debriefing

Leader: We've been using some creative activities to learn about Australia. We know more about the continent, including its geography, natural resources, people, and culture. If you were going to plan a trip to Australia, what things might you see from the airplane window? If you were to meet some Australians on your trip, what occupations might they have? If you were to open a zoo for Australian animals, what animals might you feature? Finally, if you were to bring back a present for your family, what might that be? Let's conclude our unit on Australia by making a collage that answers these questions. Please get art supplies from the back of the room.

ASSESSMENT: Complete the rubric shown in table A.1.

NOTE

1. Sovereign Hill Museums Association. *A Peep into the Past*. Ballarat, Australia: Sovereign Hill, 1986.

Table A.1. Rubric for Sample Lesson

	Yes	No	In part
Players used processes to reconstruct and reinterpret the past.			
Players understood that world regions have different natural resources.			
Players applied research to demonstrate appropriate creative choices.			
Players demonstrated acting skills to develop believable characters.			
Players demonstrated singing skills with rhythmic and melodic accuracy.			
Players used found sound to imitate likely sounds in an Australian environment.			
Players demonstrated careful listening and expressive speaking skills.			
Players accompanied songs with accurate strumming to the beat.			

Reflections for Journal Exploration

CHAPTER 1

A. What is the difference between a curriculum that prepares students to make a living and a curriculum that prepares students to make a life? Do the arts fit into either or both? In what ways?

B. What is the role of *thinking* in creative activities? What is the role of *creativity* in thinking activities? Give examples of each.

CHAPTER 2

A. The beginning activities in this chapter help to establish a creative climate. How might "creative climate" be defined? Why is it significant in creative drama sessions? In what ways could "creative climate" vary for groups who know each other well? Groups brought together only for a particular session? Groups with or without a prior relationship to the leader? Why is it helpful to learn about a group in advance of leading the session?

B. There is a fine line between found sound (environmental sound) music and noise. What is the difference? What are specific techniques the leader could use to help players distinguish between the two?

CHAPTER 3

A. Many of the activities in this chapter emphasize concentration, imagination, and teamwork. What behaviors will indicate that players are developing abilities in these

areas? Is concentration necessary for imagination? Is concentration necessary for teamwork? Support your opinions.

B. Some musical activities require that players perform strict imitation of what they have heard, while others require free improvisation. From a player's perspective, which activities are more difficult to execute? From a leader's perspective, which activities are more difficult to execute?

CHAPTER 4

A. In theatre, the tools of the actor are voice and body. In creative drama, some practitioners advocate working on physical rather than vocal training first. What justifies this approach? Support the position taken, while keeping in mind that theatre for young audiences is formal and product oriented and creative drama is informal and process oriented. How might this approach nevertheless be common ground for the two endeavors?

B. Because young children are highly imitative when moving to music and will often resort to movements of familiar animals or objects, there are challenges to nurturing creative responses to the music. To help guide their attention to the music as the inspiration point for movement, prepare an inventory of statements and questions that you can use to focus attention on the music during creative music activities, such as the following:

- Let your fingers dance the rhythm in this section of the music.
- Show me with your arms how the volume changes.
- What would you like to sway (feet, knees, arms, head, hands, etc.) back and forth to show the tempo?
- How many different ways can you march to express the spirit of the music? (On tiptoe, backward, swinging arms, crouched down, etc.)

CHAPTER 5

A. What strategies might the leader employ if, during a creative activity, a student engaged in attention-seeking behavior that made it difficult to develop ensemble playing?

B. Choral reading activities require team work. The individual must actively contribute to the overall performance and be sensitive to the overall group performance goals (volume, tempo, style, etc.). Sometimes a student's participation is at odds with the desired effect. How can the leader balance the nurturing of individual creative expression with the conformance to group conventions?

CHAPTER 6

A. Story creation can emanate from props, pictures, films, or real-life incidents. How might it be a good tool for reviewing players' understanding of protocols for tornado drills, fire drills, or emergency responses?

B. In any group of players, some students have more gifts and skills than others. What are the benefits of teaming talented students together for improvisations? What are the benefits of pairing special students with advanced students?

CHAPTER 7

A. Select a curricular unit that you currently teach or plan to teach. Integrate story-dramatization activities into the unit. How do these story activities support student learning? After teaching the unit, describe student involvement and identify ways in which these activities supported individual learning styles.

B. Some students who study music privately will begin to use formal notation in mapping and scoring activities. Is there any merit in having them explore untraditional notation? Support your opinion.

Further Resources

ON-LINE DRAMA AND MUSIC RESOURCES:[1]

www.aate.com

American Alliance for Theatre and Education is a professional organization for artists and educators.

www.aep-arts.org/

Arts Education Partnership is the source for the following publications: *Critical Links: Learning in the Arts and Student Academic and Social Development*; *Champions of Change: The Impact of the Arts on Learning*; *Making a Case for the Arts: How and Why the Arts are Critical to Student Achievement and Better Schools*; and *Third Space: When Learning Matters*.

www.americanfolklore.net/

A variety of stories suitable for dramatization.

artsedge.kennedy-center.org/

Arts standards, lessons, and interactive program materials for educators, students, and parents.

www.artsusa.org

Americans for the Arts addresses arts education and arts issues.

artswork.asu.edu/arts/teachers/lesson/drama/lesson/creative.html

Creative drama/improvisation projects and assessment.

www.bussongs.com

Over 2,000 songs and rhymes for children.

www.canteach.ca

Poems.

www.childdrama.com/childdrama.html

Main menu at site offers lesson plans and resources.

www.cre8tivedrama.com

A creative drama resource for teachers.

www.creativedrama.com

Lesson plans and resources for creative drama and theatre education.

www.head-start.lane.or.us/education/activities/music/songs-fingerplays.html

Finger plays suitable for singing and creative drama.

www.keepartsinschools.org

Advocacy tools, research, and resources.

www.kididdles.com

A collection of lyrics and audio accompaniments.

www.menc.org

The National Association for Music Education addresses all aspects of music education, from preschool to graduate school.

www.mosaicproject.org

Peace songs and audio examples.

munchkinsandmusic.blogspot.com/

Lessons and lesson plans for music instruction.

www.musicbulletinboards.net

A collection of songs and lyrics in PowerPoint format.

www.musicnotes.net
An inventory of songs categorized by grade levels.

www.nea.gov
The National Endowment for the Arts provides grants, a listing of state and national standards, initiatives, and resources.

www.nncc.org/Curriculum/fingerplay.html
National Network for Child Care site offering numerous finger plays.

www.pbs.org/wnet/dancin/resources/lesson_plan-t1.html
A lesson plan exploring the connection between drama and painting.

pbskids.org/zoom/activities/do/pantomime.html?print
Pantomime activities from PBS Kids.

www.powertolearn.com/teachers/lesson_activities/arts/index.shtml.
Arts lesson activities.

www.prel.org/eslstrategies/drama.html
Suggested drama strategies to use with ESL students.

www.sct.org
Educational resource guides and drama materials from the Seattle Children's Theatre.

www.songsforteaching.com
Content-related songs and audio examples.

www.suzyred.com
Content-related songs (e.g., language arts songs, multiplication songs, science songs, social studies songs); lyrics and accompaniments.

www.theteachersguide.com
A collection of lyrics and accompaniments.

www.traditionalmusic.co.uk
A collection of primarily English folk songs.

NOTE

1. Website resources are current as we write this text. Given the nature of the Web, however, some links may become broken over time if the resources are removed or relocated.

Glossary

Abstract: Difficult to attach specific qualities to, to define in ways that will mean exactly the same thing to everyone, or to represent with exactness.

Accelerando: Gradually increasing in tempo.

Accent: Stress or emphasis given to a syllable or note.

Accompaniment: Supportive background sounds that enhance the primary event, e.g., a drum accompaniment to chanting.

Analytical listener: One who goes beyond superficial hearing by listening discriminately for sound characteristics such as pitch, duration, texture, and so forth.

Attentive listener: One who pays attention to a sound source and recognizes general and apparent sounds in the foreground.

Bar: A vertical line that separates measures of musical time in notation. See **measure.**

Beat: Maintenance of a steady auditory pulse.

Beginning activities: Used as warm-ups or ice-breakers; simple activities usually designed to play in unison and relax players, focus attention, introduce the theme of the lesson, or establish rapport.

Believability: Synonymous with *honesty* and *truthfulness*, a goal for character portrayal and for executing dramatic action. Also, realistic behavior in dramatic play.

Body sounds: Noises that can be made using the mouth, voice, hands, or feet. These include such noises as clucking the tongue, hissing, humming, popping hands, clapping, and shuffling feet.

Brainstorming: A process wherein players think of as many ideas as possible, recording but not immediately evaluating them. Once a sufficient number of ideas has been generated, these are carefully considered and the best ones used.

Characters: People, animals, or personified objects whose development, relationships, and actions drive a story forward.

Characterization: The embodiment of the people, animals, or personified objects in a story.

Choral reading: Musical speech with interpretive expression.

Closed question: A question requiring only a yes or no answer.

Composition: A piece of music typically involving rhythm, melody, and form.

Concentration: The ability to develop and maintain focus, to be attentive, and to block out distractions. Necessary for a deep level of involvement with activities.

Concrete: Capable of being assigned specific and readily identifiable qualities and of being clearly represented and recognized.

Consonant harmony: A combination of pitches simultaneously performed that results in a pleasing, harmonious sound.

Contrast: The element of form that provides differences in rhythm or melody and creates interest or variety in a musical form.

Control: Related to discipline and used to establish safety, foster attentiveness and productivity, and facilitate organization. A control word, such as "freeze," is often used to start and stop action.

Dialogue: A character's means of expression, as determined by the nature of the role and the type of story. Evaluated by appropriateness for a particular character in a particular situation.

Dissonant harmony: A combination of simultaneous pitches that results in a clashing, discordant sound.

Duple meter: Sets of beats in patterns of two, such as a marching pattern of left, right; left, right.

Duration: The time value of notes, e.g., notes of short or long length.

Dynamics: Loudness or softness; volume.

Empathetic response: The ability to feel what someone else feels; to recognize and respond to another's emotional state with like feelings.

Ensemble playing: No one player is more important than another, and all work together for the good of the activity rather than for personal glory.

Evaluation: Assessment of what the players did well and what they can improve; often the basis for replay.

Expository scene: A scene in a story that *exposes* important information that the players will need in order to dramatize; may reveal information about a character's background, relationships, previous events, and the like.

Finger plays: Short poems, chants, or rhythmic activities with hand movements allowing for participation on a limited scale; generally quite simple, involving repetition and imitation. Recommended for young children.

Form: The structure or design of the music, poem, or chant; the organization created by repetition, contrast, or variation of elements of music.

Found sound: Noises that can be made with objects within the environment, for example by shaking, striking, or scraping them. Sounds can be deliberately manipulated for intended effects in composing activities.

"Freeze": A control word used to stop an action or activity and requiring players to remain stationary; also used for pacing within and between activities or as a means of maintaining or restoring order.

Fundamental movements: A set of simple body movements, such as locomotor movements of walking, running, skipping, and so forth.

Givens: Information about characters, conflict, setting, time, and manner, upon which improvisations are structured; improvisational format requires at least two from the categories of *who*, *what*, *when*, *where*, and *how*.

Hand jives: Patterns of movements and sounds made with hands that fit the meter and are used to accompany music or chants. For example, a three-movement pattern may consist of clap, snap, snap.

Imagination: Engaging the mind's eye in creative thought, picturization, or fanciful depiction.

Improvisation (dramatic): A spontaneous form of drama based upon given information, in which dialogue and action evolve during play.

Improvisation (musical): Freely invented or spontaneously composed music.

In role: Refers to the leader assuming a character and entering the dramatic play; often a means of guiding from within the action.

Individual play: One person per role.

Interlude: Music performed between acts of a play, stanzas of poems, readings, or other segments of a creative performance.

Leader: The teacher or other person guiding the session.

Leitmotif: A musical device that associates a short rhythmic and/or melodic pattern with a particular event, person, or place in orchestrating a poem, story, or composition.

Marginal listener: One who hears sounds but does not distinguish foreground from background noise and is unable to discriminate or focus on aural details.

Measure: Vertical lines that rule off bars or units of beats. For example, in 4/4 time, measure lines will separate every four beats.

Melodic direction: The movement of tones upward or downward within a tune.

Melody: The tune; a series of consecutive notes that forms a cohesive musical unit.

Meter: A pattern of beats with noticeable and regular accent. Meter can be felt in chants, rhymes, songs, music, and movements.

Meter signature or **time signature**: A set of numbers that conveys how beats are grouped and what the duration of each beat is. The upper number (*numerator*) represents how many beats are grouped in each measure. The lower number (*denominator*) represents which note value receives one beat; for example, 2 indicates a half note, 4 indicates a quarter note, etc.

Monologue: An uninterrupted flow of ideas or speech.

Name games: Simple activities designed to help acquaint the players and the leader, relax participants, and foster a creative climate.

Noisy story: A story in which each major character is assigned a sound, phrase, or sentence, and each time that character is mentioned, players respond as assigned.

Observation: The practice of seeing clearly and noting detail.

Open-ended question: A type of question requiring more than just a yes or no answer; a preferred way of stimulating in-depth thinking, probing, and imagining.

Open-ended story: An incomplete story that players can finish orally, in writing, or through dramatization.

Overture: Music performed before the opening of a story, play, reading, or other creative performance.

Pacing: Timing within activities or lessons; a quick pace is usually indicative of a high energy level, while a slower pace is associated with calmer, more reflective responses.

Pantomime: Expression of thoughts, feelings, and actions through physical means; employs the body but not the voice to communicate.

Patchen: Patting one's thighs with one's hands to produce a slapping sound.

Patterns of progression: Organizational sequences that may be found in lessons, including (1) short to long, (2) teacher-directed to student-directed, (3) simple to complex, and (4) unison to individual play.`

Phrase: A series of sounds that comprise a musical thought.

Pitch: The highness or lowness of a tone.

Players: Participants in a drama or music activity.

Playing space: Area in which creative drama and music activities occur.

Playing the moment: Response to a situation as if it were happening immediately and for the first time; based upon the premise that although a player knows the outcome of a story, the character would not.

Plot: Dramatic events and the order in which they occur.

Preview play: An advance look at a portion of the player's interpretation; used to check for valid ideas capable of being enacted.

Prop: Shortened form of *property*; refers to items used by a character.

Quadruple meter: Sets of beats in patterns of four.

Quieting activity: Used to calm and relax; often found at the end of lessons or interspersed between activities demanding high levels of energy.

Repetition: The repeating of a rhythm or melody to create unity.

Replay: Engaging in an activity again in order to improve play, involve new players, or explore other interpretations and ideas.

Rhythm: A series of notes, often of differing durations, that constitute the flow of music through time.

Ritardando: Gradually decreasing in tempo.

Role playing: Allows players to examine issues, try on characters without negative consequence, engage in problem solving, and explore feelings; uses an improvisational format.

Rondo: The form or organization of a composition in which a certain theme recurs after contrasting sections. For example, theme A repeats after themes B, C, and D to result in the following structure of themes: ABACADA.

Round: A type of performance in which two or more groups perform the same music with one group starting before the other enters.

Score: Written notation mapping music that is heard or music that is to be performed. For sound pieces, the notation is typically pictorial and graphic. For traditional music, standard notation is used.

Sensory awareness: Cognition of properties related to seeing, hearing, tasting, feeling, and smelling.

Sidecoaching: Descriptive commentary by the leader, designed to deepen players' involvement; given in the form of statements, open-ended questions, and rhetorical questions, either individually or on a group basis.

Solo: One player performing alone.

Soundscape: The overall mood or effect of a piece of music.

Story creation: Creating stories orally, in writing, or through dramatization.

Story dramatization: Bringing a story to life through words and actions; a complex procedure in creative drama involving analysis, dramatization, evaluation, and replay.

Student directed: Players have more responsibility for the guidance and success of the endeavor than does the leader.

Style: A manner of musical expression with characteristics that form a specific genre or category, such as jazz, classical, folk, ethnic, or other types of music.

Subtext: The thoughts and emotions underlying the dialogue.

Teacher directed: The teacher bears primary responsibility for planning and leading activities; often prevalent in early experiences.

Tempo: Fastness or slowness; speed.

Texture: Thinness or thickness of simultaneous sounds, e.g., a single flute texture vs. an orchestra texture of twenty different instrumental sounds.

Timbre or **tone color**: The characteristic sound of the voice or instrument that gives it its unique personality. For example, the tone color of a tuba sounds much heavier, thicker, and lower than that of a piccolo.

Time signature: See **meter signature**.

Tone color: See **timbre**.

Triple meter: Sets of beats in patterns of three, such as a waltz pattern of "um, pah, pah."

Try-on: A procedure in which players imagine that they are a character engaged in some bit of action that may or may not be mentioned in a story being dramatized; provides an opportunity for all to play the character and allows the leader to preview interpretations.

Unison play: All players involved together and participating in an activity at the same time.

Visualization: The use of mental imagery in developing imaginative and appropriate dramatic responses.

Index

About the Authors

Janet E. Rubin, Ph.D., is professor of theatre at Saginaw Valley State University. She has served as national president of the American Alliance for Theatre and Education, as a panelist for the National Endowment for the Arts and Michigan Council for the Arts and Cultural Affairs, and as a board member for the Michigan Humanities Council. In addition, Dr. Rubin has served as educator in residence at the University of Mysore (India) and at Ballarat College of Advanced Education (Victoria, Australia). She is the recipient of numerous awards, including the Earl L. Warrick Award for Excellence in Research, the Rush Distinguished Lectureship, and the Barstow Humanities Seminar Directorship.

Margaret Merrion serves as professor and dean of the College of Fine Arts at Western Michigan University. She began her teaching career in the public and private schools of Chicago. After earning a masters and doctoral degrees in music education at the University of Missouri, she taught K–8 vocal music at the University of Northern Iowa's Price Laboratory School as well as music methods in the School of Music at the University of Northern Iowa and Ball State University. She is a former president of the International Council of Fine Arts Deans.